Sandy

Hook Massacre

When Seconds Count — Police are Minutes Away

by DOUG GILES

and

CLASHDAILY.COM

Contributors

Published by White Feather Press. (www.whitefeatherpress.com)

ISBN 978-1-61808-059-2

Printed in the United States of America

Cover design by Doug Giles and David Bugnon of mobopolis.com"

White Feather Press

Reaffirming Faith in God, Family, and Country!

Dedication-

This book is dedicated to the culture warriors who write for my website, ClashDaily.com.

Molon Labe.

Publisher's Note

When Doug Giles came to me with the idea for publishing a politically incorrect commentary about gun control, mass shootings and the Sandy Hook Massacre I thought about it briefly and then asked him, "Do you realize how much flack you're going to take for this?" Doug didn't bat an eye. He knew. And so did I.

I agreed to publish this book simply because it was the right thing to do. People have been fed so much falsehood from the mainstream media about guns that a candid and truthful commentary had to be published just to inject some balance. So this is a pro-gun defense of the right to keep and bear arms in light of all the crazy mass shootings going on the past twenty years.

But let me warn you right out of the box. If you believe the "militia" is the National Guard, you won't like this book. If you believe an AR-15 fires like a machine gun, then stop reading. If you are convinced the Second Amendment is all about hunting, then go back to watching *American Idol* and reading the *National Enquirer*. However, if you love the Second Amendment and want the right to protect your family from both civilian and governmental criminals, then this is the book for you. Keep reading.

There's one important thing I've done in this book that you'll notice as you read. I've taken the liberty of deleting all the names of mass murderers, and in their place you'll see "He who shall not be named" or "~~Name Deleted~~". This is one publisher who won't be glorifying sick, murdering bastards and enshrining them in print, thus guaranteeing their legacy. As far as I'm concerned, mass shooters can burn anonymously in hell.

Instead, let us remember the victims; let us pray for them; let us dedicate our lives to double-tapping the center of bad-guy exposed mass until they go down to the ground, nameless, unglorified, unwept and unsung. I know. It sounds harsh, but these are harsh times.

MOLON LABE

Skip Coryell
President, White Feather Press

Introduction

The book *Sandy Hook Massacre: When Seconds Count – Police Are Minutes Away* is a compendium of columns that were originally penned by my writers and I over at ClashDaily.com after the avoidable massacre at Sandy Hook Elementary occurred in Newtown, Connecticut on December 14th, 2012.

The book, as you will see, is laid out in chronological order. I chose to arrange it this way in order to show our response to the initial shooting and the victims, the deranged killer, the media melee and the creepy unconstitutional political overreach that this tragedy spawned.

There are many lessons to be drawn from the awful Newtown, CT school shooting. Unfortunately, most of the media and political Left came up with the wrong ones. Not us over at ClashDaily.com, however. In the wake of this horror, we offer a robust defense of American citizens' "right to keep and bear arms" and a common sense analysis of the actual answers to societal violence.

Going forward, I believe this book will be a significant resource for those interested in this vital, Constitutional issue.

Doug Giles
CEO of ClashDaily.com
Miami, Florida

Contents

Look, even the best Rambo like police force equipped to the teeth, driving Vipers and descending en masse on a school in Black Hawk helicopters could not have responded fast enough to kill this piece of crap. But a fast thinking, well-trained teacher could have.

New Rule: Teachers Should Be Allowed to Carry Guns

Written By Doug Giles

16 December 2012

My heart is sick. I feel so sorry for the children that were murdered, as well as the parents and loved ones of the slain kids and teachers at Sandy Hook Elementary School in Newtown. Connecticut—and all of us here in the U.S., who still have a soul, pray for those whose lives were just senselessly shattered.

But imagine if at least one teacher (with a concealed weapons permit) had their .40 caliber Glock with them, locked and loaded, when this weed began his murderous mayhem today on the Sandy Hook Elementary School campus? What would have happened differently?

Would idiot boy have been able to slay 20 children and 6 teachers? I doubt it. But then again . . . who knows?

However, I'm guessing that this terminal turd might not have dealt out as much death (if any) if the good guy with the gun drew down on him and doubled tapped the center mass of this jackass with a couple of jacketed hollow points.

Unfortunately, there was no concealed weapon in the possession of a teacher to stop this satanic weed from taking root because guns are disallowed on campus. Correct me if I'm wrong, but haven't the majority of the mass murders within the US in the last 20-30 years been in the Gun Free Zones?

Gun Free Zones turn the people who inhabit such places into sitting ducks for insane whack jobs with death wishes. I know, some schools have campus cops and security systems however, that line of defense brings zero comfort to most parents if serious bullet flying $#*& starts hitting the fan in one of their kid's classes.

Look, even the best Rambo like police force equipped to the teeth, driving Vipers and descending en masse on a school in Black Hawk helicopters could not have responded fast enough to kill this piece of crap. But a fast thinking, well-trained teacher could have.

I hate to seem pessimistic, but given this current "poor me" entitlement culture, I don't see an atmospheric break in this violent weather pattern. I guarantee that even as I type and our nation weeps, there is, somewhere in the United States of Political Correctness, some disenfranchised dipstick making plans on how he can trump the latest slaughter. Chilling.

Call me simple. Call me a redneck. Call me whatever the hell you wanna call me—but until we allow credible and licensed, proven and protective teachers to carry a weapon on campus, we will see this murderous madness occur again and again and again.

Matter of fact, if I owned and operated Doug Giles Elementary School I would mandate that all my teachers be weapons trained and carry a live pistol openly at all times. I bet that 100% of the parents who lost their children today wished that their child's teacher had a gun in order to defend their now deceased child.

We can't afford to rely on security systems or chunky security guards with golf carts, pepper spray, whistles and plastic badges to safeguard against these armed little death dealers from hell

The reality is that this stuff goes down when you least expect it, and as long as schools don't have some armed teachers and faculty that have been properly trained and equipped to kill the post-pubescent perps, the more we will continue to carry innocent children out of their classrooms in black body bags. Call me weird, but in every school shooting there should be only one casualty, namely the gun-wielding culprit who commenced the chaos, and not your bystanding Crayon carrying kid or their teachers.

About Doug Giles

Doug Giles is the man behind ClashDaily.com. In addition to driving ClashDaily.com, Giles is a popular columnist on Townhall.com and the author of the book Raising Righteous & Rowdy Girls.

Doug's articles have also appeared on several other print and online news sources, including The Washington Times, The Daily Caller, Fox Nation, USA Today, The Wall Street Journal, The Washington Examiner, The Blaze, American Hunter Magazine and ABC News.

He's been a frequent guest on the Fox News Channel and Fox Business Channel as well as many nationally syndicated radio shows across the nation — which, he believes, officially makes him a super hero.

In addition, Doug is an occasional guest host on New York City's WABC (The Jason Mattera Show) and he is a weekly guest, every Friday at 7:45am[et], on America's Morning News (155 markets).

Giles and his wife Margaret have two daughters: Hannah, who devastated ACORN with her 2009 nation shaking undercover videos, and Regis who is an NRA columnist, huntress and Second Amendment activist.

DG's interests include guns, big game hunting, big game fishing, fine art, cigars, helping wounded warriors, and being a big pain in the butt to people who dislike God and the USA.

Read more Doug Giles at www.clashdaily.com.

Without dispute, a handgun in the classroom is a blazingly politically-incorrect answer for this era — a completely sensible one, if knee-jerk, anti-gun emotionalism can be put aside, but still paralyzingly controversial.

Geraldo Rivera (Sort of) Admits: Guns Needed in Schools

Written By Steve Pauwels

16 December 2012

It was, likely, unintentional, but mere hours following the Newtown, CT slaughter of a classroom full of children and half-a-dozen school personnel, TV journalist Geraldo Rivera conceded that guns ought to be in America's public schools. Near the wrap-up of a tearful discussion about the mass-murder, the colorful Fox News fixture avowed to host Bill O'Reilly that, hereafter, "every school" ought to have a full-time police officer present to foreclose any repeat of Friday's bloody travesty.

An hour later on Sean Hannity's program, former New York City detective Bo Dietl essentially echoed Geraldo's prescription (tossing in the retired/off-duty policeman/hired security officer option, as well).

Again, although it was probably not the point of the pseudo-Liberal Rivera — perhaps not even of the more politically conservative Dietl — it's not a radical notion at all to move from the armed-cop-at-school antidote to the conclusion that … well, at least some school employees ought to be allowed to arrive daily at the school-house door packing heat. Maybe even encouraged to do so?

Think about it: an on-premises blue suit can be trusted with protecting our children, resorting to a 9 mm if necessary — but not a handful of thoroughly-vetted, rigorously trained teachers, counselors, administrators or custodians who already are charged with their guardianship? I suppose if one occupies sports-announcer Bob Costas' realm in which gun-toting citizens aren't functionally up to bearing arms against imminent danger, a handgun hefting educator is a possibility not to be contemplated.

Remember, Costas recently stood by his unblanching insistence that an armed audience member at the Aurora, Colorado movie theater massacre only would have augmented the body count. It's a view of human beings against which Toqueville darkly cautioned two hundred years ago: regular folks " stupifie[d] … reduced to nothing better than a flock of timid and industrious animals, of which the government is the shepherd."

Can't trust "we the people" to take account of our own lives! — better await the "professionals" and "experts" who know best how to protect us, provide for us, corral us.

Why would a school's single, easily identifiable, "official" gun-carrier be preferred to three or four, perhaps generally anonymous, adult staff fully equipped to violently defend vulnerable students if necessary? Let's be frank: all a methodical, sufficiently prepped malefactor has to do is play innocent until he finds the unsuspecting police officer; and then cut him/her down. And where would we be then? Right back to the situation that obtained in New-town, CT, December 14, 2012: a building full of helpless victims with no one to shield them

Metal detectors at every educational facility! Some clamor. How about a TSA style arrangement at the entrances of our schools? Once more — not meaning to be morbid, only realistic — with a modicum of forethought, the thorough predator can defeat such. He only has to dispatch the technologi-cal barriers by dispatching those operating them. Dead gatekeepers can't use fancy gadgets to keep out the bad guys.

What these gruesomely unsparing scenarios all reinforce is, bottom line, a fifth grade art teacher or fifty-five year old janitor, experienced in point, aim, squeeze, can stop the most determined beast in his tracks even when all the other, more conventional barriers have failed.

What Rivera and Dietl both affirmed, whether they meant to or not, is — despite all the worthy lionizing of courageous teachers who keep their wits about them and effectively shuttle their students out back doors or into hiding places while the rounds are flying — oftentimes, physical counterforce ends up being called for.

A bespectacled educator hurling a fire extinguisher at a gun-wielding mon-ster? A normally mild-mannered administrator going after a snarling cutthroat with a letter opener or knitting needle? Nobody would flinch at such turn of events — in fact, the heroes would be marched down main street and covered with confetti.

But suggest these same men or women ought to be urged to keep a firearm handy? The sophisticated types gasp — the same sophisticated types raging today: How can horrors like Newtown unfold in our day?!?

Without dispute, a handgun in the classroom is a blazingly politically-incorrect answer for this era — a completely sensible one, if knee-jerk, anti-gun emotionalism can be put aside, but still paralyzingly controversial.

But, so what? The "respectable" solutions keep falling short. Maybe "controversial' and "politically incorrect" just mean: gutsy but needful. Maybe they just mean: ugly but essential.

No educational professional, of course, should be required to carry a firearm to work; but word ought to go out that any decision in that direction would be welcomed. How about every school system's asking that staff volunteer to fulfill a minimal quota of licensed carriers? Paying for mandatory training in responsible firearm usage? Offering a salary bonus for those who step up to this solemn but vital responsibility?

Only the local superintendent and principal or top administrator need know who compose this thin, pedagogical line — and most importantly, the criminals shouldn't know. That element of uncertainty alone would serve as a doughty deterrent.

Teachers equipped, practically, to kill if need be? It's an unpleasant exigency, a nasty provision. Yet, perhaps, Newtown, CT will prompt us to reconsider some previously unfathomable responses.

Founding Father James Madison noted, "If men were angels, no government would be necessary." I'm minded to paraphrase him: if men were angels, neither would schools ever have to fear maniacs; nor the good guys need weapons to thwart them.

But men aren't angels, are they. If we didn't get that a few days ago, surely we do now.

About the Author

Steve Pauwels is managing editor of ClashDaily.com

Double steel security doors, security cameras and a standard practice of "buzzing" in visitors to access public school buildings offers only a false sense of security and does not ensure anyone's safety against armed lunatics.

"GUN-FREE" SCHOOL-ZONE LAW IS A FAILURE

Written By Loretta Baughan

17 December 2012

As last Friday's tragic massacre at a Connecticut elementary school clearly demonstrates, the Gun-Free School Zone law doesn't work because crazed, evil lunatics hell-bent on murdering innocents don't give a damn about any law.

Pardon my French.

Right on cue, anti-gun activists are trying to exploit and politicalize this horrendous mass murder to advance their obsession of banning guns. Why should millions of law-abiding gun owners be punished because of a few mentally deranged individuals?

It's nonsense.

Guns don't kill, people do. Sick, evil, twisted, fame-seeking cowards who plan to kill innocents are drawn to places where they know guns are prohibited. Eliminate guns and evil people determined to commit murder will use knives, baseball bats, hammers, rocks, bombs or something else – just as they do in countries where gun ownership is tightly controlled or prohibited.

Has outlawing drugs stopped drug abuse? No. Outlaw guns and only the criminals will have them.

Friday's horrific massacre was without rhyme or reason. Who, in their right mind, would victimize innocent children and dedicated teachers as this monster did? Reportedly, he was mentally disturbed, but that's no excuse. It's still an issue of personal responsibility. The murderer is responsible, not the gun.

I cannot begin to fathom the horror faced by these precious souls trapped inside the elementary school as they awaited their deaths. It's unthinkable. This kind of heinous, senseless violence makes my blood boil, especially knowing a well-trained and armed adult at the school could have prevented or ended the executions.

Double steel security doors, security cameras and a standard practice of "buzzing" in visitors to access public school buildings offers only a false sense of security and does not ensure anyone's safety against armed lunatics. Many school buildings are entirely without security measures. Regardless, a person who's determined to gain entrance can likely do so by breaking out a ground-level window or entering by an unsecured service door.

Connecticut has a gun law which allows people to carry at schools, but only with the school district's approval. Since many administrators and school boards are dominated by progressive-minded, anti-gun types, I would be surprised if anyone in Connecticut has been granted permission. Putting the power of approval into the hands of school districts or boards is a cop-out on the part of legislators trying to appease the education industry instead of doing everything possible to make schools safe.

Once again, the police arrived on the scene too late to prevent the mayhem. God bless our law enforcement officers. But had someone been armed at Sandy Hook Elementary School, this needless tragedy may have been averted and innocent lives saved.

Michigan's new legislation awaiting Governor Snyder's signature will allow concealed carry licensees, who receive additional training, an exemption to bring a handgun into schools and other public locations designated as "gun-free zones".

Similar laws are needed in every state.

Many schools have ex-military teachers, custodians and administrators on staff and lots of folks who hunt. What do you want to bet they would be standing in line to volunteer for training to carry at schools?

I'd like to suggest training in the form of a course offered periodically by local county sheriff departments which include a hands-on, shooting range requirement. This would permit the local law enforcement agencies to know who may be armed at a particular school and have the opportunity to instruct the person(s) how best to deal with various scenarios. The valuable course would not only provide the attendees with knowledge to deal with threats, but give them the confidence to be able to take effective action, if, God forbid, ever needed.

By premeditated design, these tragic murders happen where least expected and without warning. After Newtown's massacre, we cannot be lulled into thinking any place is "safe". We can't afford to be unprepared. In this increasingly uncivilized world in which we live, we cannot deny trained and licensed citizens their right to self-protection and to serve the public safety as a line of defense in protecting our school children.

Lives may depend upon it.

ABOUT THE AUTHOR

Loretta Baughan is a conservative school board member who home-schooled her children and supports parental choice. Over the past twenty-five years, she's been self-employed as a professional photographer, webdesigner and raising hunting spaniels.

Evil is with us, but so is good. In the midst of every tragedy like this there are always stories of heroes. For every evil-minded individual dedicated to taking lives, there are several dedicated to saving them.

THE CONNECTICUT SCHOOL SHOOTING – WHAT ARE YOU GOING TO DO ABOUT IT?

Written By Irwin Podhajser

18 December 2012

The politicians on both side of the aisle will take opportunities to add political arguments to the tragedy in Connecticut. Gun control, violence in video games and the state of our mental health system will be front and center for the next couple of weeks.

I'm not here to say that our country doesn't need healthy debate on these issues and others, I'm just saying that all these issues have nothing to do with the underlying problem that was the cause of this horrific tragedy.

What is this underlying problem? Evil! Yes it is that simple and that complex. Evil is with us, it has always been with us and it always will be with us.

Do you know what the worst school killing in US history was? It was the Bath School Disaster in 1925. Andrew Kehoe killed 45 kids and adults using a bomb. That's right no gun and well before the age of video games. Violence is not a new phenomenon and to pretend that it is is to ignore hard truths and to believe that we can stop future killings by changing some rules.

Evil is with us, but so is good. In the midst of every tragedy like this there are always stories of heroes. For every evil-minded individual dedicated to taking lives, there are several dedicated to saving them. This event shocked us because something like this doesn't happen in an upscale town. The hard reality is that thousands of children die every week throughout this world through violence, neglect and starvation. We have become desensitized towards it until it breaks through some "invincible barrier".

Just a week ago I told a young man that in this world, there are takers and there are givers. Everyone must choose which one they will be. You are either dedicating your life to taking and helping the forces of evil or you are a giver and are building walls to hold the evil at bay.

I was fortunate enough to know Dana Scott. She is the sister of Rachel Scott who died in the Columbine shooting. Rachel was a giver. She was a light in this world and to the very end she proclaimed allegiance to that light even while evil taunted her at the point of the gun that took her life. The evil that was unleashed on that day in Colorado lives on, but so does the light and with more than tens years of perspective, the light has outshone the evil.

Dana, as well as Rachel's dad and brother, looked that evil in the face and rather than crumble under its weight, they rose and embraced the light Rachel fought for and through their efforts a message of hope and love came out of that tragedy, just like it will from this current tragedy. [Editor: Rachel's tragic but courageous death became "the inspiration for Rachel's Challenge, a nationwide school outreach program for the prevention of teen violence, based on her life and writings".]

It all comes down to the individual. It all comes down to what each of us chooses to do with our lives.

What type of person will we decide to be?

Did you know that in total darkness, even one flame can be seen for miles. Darkness cannot exist where there is light even one tiny flame. Do you want to honor those that died and die each day? Do you want to help prevent more from dying? Then don't just spend a week in mourning. Rise up and make a difference. Give more than you take and, in the little things of life, be the bearer of light.

Evil is with us and will always be with us. Children like those in that school die every day because evil is with us. Wipe away the tears of this week and decide what YOU are going to do about it.

ABOUT THE AUTHOR

Irwin has had an eclectic line of careers including 15 years as a Miami youth pastor, media buyer and television executive. He is currently the President of DrTV Network which is a multi-level television network dedicated towards healthy living. He also serves as Chairman for The Advanced Television Broadcasting Alliance.

If we want gun control then fine, let's make sure the government has every one of our teachers properly trained, strapped, and ready to put a .223 round between the eyes of another Columbine, Virginia Tech, or Sandy Hook wannabe should the occasion arise.

SCHOOLS SHOULD DEMAND GUN-READY TEACHERS

Written By Andres Ortiz

18 December 2012

Before I go off into a passionate ranting about how ill prepared schools are today towards the defense of their staff and students, I would just like to say that I am in prayer for those directly affected by the massacre that took place last week in Sandy Hook Elementary. I cannot begin to imagine the grief that these families must be going through right now; the loss of a child is always painful but this kind of massacre is not even seen in horror movies.

After talking to my circle of friends about what could have been done to prevent such a tragedy, I believe I came to a nearly foolproof solution that will not only keep the children safe but also increase the quality of our education system: every teacher should be properly trained and certified to handle a firearm in case of an emergency of immediate harm to their students. Every public school teacher is in charge of dozens of kids a day, and from my recollection I don't think a quarter of my teachers were ready to end a massacre before the killer ever raised his gun at a student.

Parents are entrusting their children to the public school system for the majority of the week, and what is their promise to keep the children safe? "Security" guards, cameras, and an army of teachers of which half can barely run a mile without having a heart attack. You must be kidding; those only serve a sadistic killer two additional benefits: more targets and their shooting spree being immortalized on YouTube.

If you don't believe that this is a pressing matter that should be taken on then let's consider how often school shootings happen. According to ABC News, there have been 14 school shootings since 1997. By the way, the article is titled *"Some of the Deadliest School Shootings."* Reluctantly I can assure you, if we keep going down the path we are on now then we have not yet seen the climax of massacres in the United States.

If our preparation to prevent these kinds of tragedies is to have a handful of police officers on campus at all times then we are still leaving classrooms unchecked and unprotected. I remember when I was in school the only safety measure I ever saw take place was random bag checks, and by that I mean my bag was maybe checked twice throughout all of high school. Also, I went to the same high school that Trayvon Martin went to and I don't say that with pride.

Then there are security guards, which are a joke. The only purpose they serve is to check who is skipping class or making out under the staircase. I remember in my senior year, when I was fed up with school, I would casually walk out during lunch time a block to my car, drive to get food and come back. Not once did a "security" guard or an administrator take notice of me leaving and coming back. What if I had been a demented psychopath walking out of school to grab my armory and bring it back to massacre the student body? But we had a "gun-free" zone sign right as you entered the school so I guess I would have just canceled my psychopathic plans at that point, right?

If we want gun control then fine, let's make sure the government has every one of our teachers properly trained, strapped, and ready to put a .223 round between the eyes of another Columbine, Virginia Tech, or Sandy Hook wannabe should the occasion arise.

Moreover, this kind of tragedy should be a reflection of what we are teaching the next generation about murder and accountability. If we teach them that they are nothing but chemical accidents and that the only thing humans have over monkeys is less hair and straighter limbs, then don't be surprised when they go ape [crap] and shoot up their parents and a school.

If the shooting at Sandy Hook proved anything it was not that we need more gun control or that anti-bullying campaigns should go into overdrive. From this we have learned that no one is safe, and we should prepare as such.

Lastly, it is not wise to blame God for a tragedy that happened in an institution where even the mention of His name is cause for suspension.

ABOUT THE AUTHOR

Andres Ortiz is the video producer for ClashDaily.com, he is also a musician and much involved in the Christian underground scene filming concerts, interviews, and short documentaries for international touring acts. He has been a devoted member of Clash Church since late 2006. His projects include: Polycarp Media, The Saving, and Clash Worship.

Criminals clearly have no interest in obeying the laws, that's why they are criminals. However, to say that they pay no attention to laws is simply not true. Why else do mass shootings happen in precisely the places where guns are outlawed? The criminals know that there will be no one shooting back.

CRIMINALS LURED TO "GUN-FREE" SCHOOL ZONES

Written By Mike Troxel

18 December 2012

It's time. Time to arm teachers and staff members at our public schools. The worst mass shootings in our country's history have all occurred in supposed "gun free" zones. They were – for everyone but the criminals who didn't care about obeying the law, or town ordinances or the wishes of the property owners.

Thomas Jefferson said it fairly succinctly in his *"Legal Commonplace Book"* when he included this,

> *"Laws that forbid the carrying of arms ... disarm only those who are neither inclined nor determined to commit crimes. Such laws make things worse for the assaulted and better for the assailants; they serve rather to encourage than prevent homicides, for an unarmed man may be attacked with greater confidence than an armed one."*

Criminals clearly have no interest in obeying the laws, that's why they are criminals. However, to say that they pay no attention to laws is simply not true. Why else do mass shootings happen in precisely the places where guns are outlawed? The criminals know that there will be no one shooting back.

There are over 2 million defensive handgun uses each year. Most of these result in the attempted crime being thwarted without the intended victim ever having to fire a shot. Why? Because an unarmed man may be attacked with greater confidence than an armed one, and these intended victims were armed.

Believe it or not, many armed criminals cease their crimes when merely confronted with armed opposition. Why? Because the mental aspect of the confidence with which they can act is challenged, and many of them decide to cease their intended actions.

A story you didn't hear about last week was about the way the mall shooting in Oregon ended. I'm sure you probably heard about the mall shooting, but what you almost certainly didn't hear about was 22 year old concealed carrier Nick Meli who was at the mall with a friend when he heard the gun shots, took cover, drew his gun, had the shooter in his sights and then didn't fire.

KGW News Channel 8 covered the story and interviewed him. Meli saw someone move behind the shooter and was afraid that if he fired and missed, he might injure or kill an innocent person. For that reason, he remained behind cover. As for the shooter, upon seeing that he was now opposed by an armed citizen, his next bullet was for himself and there the incident ended without any further loss of life.

Given the great incidence with which shootings with a massive loss of life happen in schools as compared to other locations, as well as given the high propensity with which these schools are "gun free" zones where teachers are unable to defend themselves and their students, it's time to stop putting them in danger by denying them the basic ability of self-defense against armed individuals with no regard for the law or the well being of others.

The Supreme Court has held on numerous occasions that law enforcement is under no obligation to protect anyone, from anything, and that the burden of responsibility lies with the individual. For the love of all that is good and holy, let's stop denying our teachers and school staff the basic necessities to protect themselves and our children from those who would do them harm.

About the Author

Mike Troxel is a right-wing, rabble rousing, Constitution loving, Tea Party starting trouble maker. He threw his locality's first ever Tea Party event, helped start and served as his local Tea Party's Vice-President. He is currently the Communications Chair for the Virginia Tea Party Patriots Federation and was accidentally elected to public office, by write-in, on election day. His interests include kayaking, rock climbing, chess, assassinating large woodland creatures with his bow, and over a decade of mixed martial arts. He holds an undergraduate degree in Print Journalism and a graduate degree in Business Administration.

When we work arduously to instill in our kids the "fact" that they evolved from slime ... and slime has no purpose, why are we stunned when they destroy some of the most vulnerable among us?

NEWTOWN TRAGEDY: AS THEY MOURN, WILL WE FINALLY DISCERN?

Written By Audrey Russo

18 December 2012

> *"Don't ever take a fence down until you know the reason it was put up."*
> *–G. K. Chesterton*

As the details of the deceased perp, ~~Name Deleted~~, emerge from the Dec. 14th shooting in Newtown, CT, and we collectively exhale … we need to approach this horror that occurred with sound minds and wisdom to move ahead.

This is clearly not the time for knee-jerk reactions. Bad laws are made without reason and based upon emotion.

What we experienced was pure evil … the result of a sin-tainted world rearing its grotesque facade. This was not the best that humanity has to offer, but the underbelly of the human soul. Could it have been stopped … a cruel thought to those suffering from unfathomable loss.

A plethora of questions come to mind: It appears from some reports, the mother of the perp may have realized there was something wrong with her son. If that was the case, why did he have access to her firearms and who taught him to shoot so accurately? The murderer had been diagnosed with Asperger's syndrome, a mild form of autism characterized by social awkwardness. No studies have been done to determine a link between Asperger's and violence, BUT doctors say that patients with Asperger's appear to lack empathy for others because they can't understand emotions. All this will be discussed interminably in the medical community. But a far greater issue is overlooked when such cold-hearted acts are committed…

Our Founders were prescient men. Their language and reasoning appears light-years beyond our own today. One of their documents, our Declaration of Independence, guarantees citizens the following:

> *"We hold these truths to be self-evident, that all men are created equal, that they are endowed by their Creator with certain unalienable Rights, that among these are Life, Liberty and the pursuit of Happiness."*

Despite what some may argue ... these ARE rights and in proper order. The first being Life. We cannot decide when life begins by changing the nomenclature of a human to meet our desires. The moment we attempt to get around someone else's right to life ... breaching the fence erected there for the protection of all ... we pay a heavy price.

A good self-examination concerning this horrific event is necessary as a culture, if we are ever to move ahead. Let's ask ourselves:

- When we work arduously to instill in our kids the "fact" that they evolved from slime ... and slime has no purpose, why are we stunned when they destroy some of the most vulnerable among us?

- Why are we not questioning our own reasoning regarding the value of life itself? Is it rational or reasonable to say that a worthless piece of tissue suddenly becomes priceless ... on an imperfect human whim? And if that is our mindset, why would we consider punishing a young adult, reared in that frame of reference, for acting out of that foundation?

What the deceased perp, ~~Name Deleted~~, committed was pure unadulterated evil. An act that has ripped the hearts of many with a wound that will never truly heal. Everyday, holiday or not, will bring a sting like acid into this open wound ... and will haunt the mind with questions of "what ifs", "I should have'" and "if I had only".

Are we our brother's keeper? As individuals, yes ... not as a Big Brother government watching in a power-grab attempt. There is culpability in the culture ... those who make government, NOT the government itself ... for the mindset of a person who slaughters the innocent. The murderer's mental state may have been awry ... as some witnesses have attested to ... but regardless, he was still making decisions based upon a foundation that not ALL life is precious ... and if some can make that choice, why can't he?

G. K. Chesterton once said: "Art, like morality, consists of drawing the line somewhere."

The line for life was drawn long ago. If we continue to ignore that line … tragically in our myopia … we will suffer many more active shooters, and far worse.

Will we finally discern the error of our ways? For the sake of those torn apart by evil, I pray so…

ABOUT THE AUTHOR

Audrey Russo is the Host of the weekly REELTalk Radio Show and the co-host of WOMANTalk Radio Show. She handles Middle East Issues/National Security/Terrorism for their eZine and writes on foreign affairs for The Examiner.com. She guests on several radio shows including The Rick Amato Show, The Simon Conway Show, The Pat Campbell Show and The Mike Wiley Show. Audrey is the Managing Editor for the online opinion journal Ediblog.com. Her articles can also be read at The Center for Changing Worldviews and the Gold Coast Chronicle as well as other online journals. She is also an active member of the NYC performing arts community as a singer and actor.

And, in case you didn't know, there was another attack in a Chinese Elementary school on the exact day of the Sandy Hook tragedy where 22 children were slashed with a knife by another demented individual. Guns are not the dilemma.

LIONESS ALERT: MOM DEMANDS ARMED GUARD ON HER KID'S CAMPUS

Written By Mary Gjertsen

18 December 2012

The images of the twenty children and six adults from Sandy Hook Elementary continue to rattle the minds of people nationwide … particularly parents. Let me just say, as a parent myself, I was outraged. What in the world was ~~Name Deleted~~ thinking when he decided to march into an elementary school and shoot, repeatedly, twenty bright-eyed and energetic kindergartners and first graders? And he didn't stop there. He even attempted to go a step further and attack other classrooms. But because of the heroic actions of many teachers, some of whom did not survive, he was not able to do so. It wasn't until police arrived, approximately 20 minutes later, that the murderer would take his own life. I don't know about you, but my heart aches for the children and families at Sandy Hook Elementary in Newtown, Connecticut.

As a mother, this horrifying tragedy hit way too close to home for me. My first reaction was to immediately remove my children from school and homeschool them. But that doesn't solve the issue at hand. I may still decide to homeschool them in the future. But for now, I've made it my priority to ensure that security measures are established at their school.

Following the Columbine High School massacre in 1999, schools were required to keep all doors locked during school hours. This was a great initial step. But as we've unfortunately learned, this by itself will not deter a crazed lunatic on a mission.

How about armed personnel for instance? If it costs us a few more tax dollars to guarantee that our children are safe, don't you think it is worth it? Call me crazy, but maybe, just maybe if armed workers, security guards, or police officers were present, the tragedy at Sandy Hook Elementary may have never happened.

I've heard the argument. If we get rid of guns, we get rid of the problem. That's bull-honky. Let's unarm the innocent person and school so that a dill weed like ~~Name Deleted~~ can obtain an illegal weapon and march right into another schoolyard and kill dozens more; all because schools were unprepared. And, in case you didn't know, there was another attack in a Chinese Elementary school on the exact day of the Sandy Hook tragedy where 22 children were slashed with a knife by another demented individual. Guns are not the dilemma.

So, what do you the parent do now? First and foremost, since you conceived and birthed that amazing creation, you have been called to love and protect that child. Start by making a phone call or emailing your child's school. Find out what they have decided to do to ensure that your child is safe. If their response is not satisfactory, demand that they take further action. I did. So did many other concerned parents. And when I pulled up to pick up my little laddets from school on Monday, I was thrilled to see that there were ARMED police personnel on the school property.

According to an ABC news report on school safety, "safety officials do not agree yet on what teachers and students should do when a homicidal gunman invades their school." This is an abomination. We must ensure that the security measures are permanently established immediately.

So parent, please get off the cellphone and get rid of your distractions. As you pull up to the school parking lot, pay attention to the surroundings. And get involved in your child's school and its policies. I challenge you to make a difference and take that initial step.

ABOUT THE AUTHOR

Mary is a stay-at-home mother of three beautiful kids and she heads up ClashChurch.com's children's ministry.

"Here, in our little house in a small town not much different than Newtown, we will pray. We will pray for goodness and for peace and for clarity. We will pray for the families. We will pray for the school."

Newtown, CT Massacre
One of Those "Moments"

Written by Pauline Wolak

19 December 2012

It's likely a moment that will change everything in America. The actions of one man at 9:30 in the morning on a Friday will define us as a nation. In the coming weeks committees will convene in Washington. We'll have debates about gun control, violent video games, and the removal of God from schools, the breakdown of traditional families, mental illness, and lack of care for the mentally ill. Blame will be placed where it doesn't belong in order to give forward momentum to personal and political agendas. The war on "fill in the blank" will go on for months.

Two moments reminded me how unimportant anyone's agenda is at this very moment. The first came last night when President Obama read the names of the twenty smallest victims. Hearing the sobs of the families in the background was gut-wrenching. I cannot begin to imagine the pain. I pray I never have to experience it.

Then this morning happened. Just like every Monday, we woke up for school. Breakfast, uniforms on, coats, backpacks, and out the door we went. The closer I got to school, the more I thought about the parents in Newtown. They dropped their children off on a day much like today, never knowing it would be the last time they'd see them. They, too, went about their morning routines, never knowing what was to come.

A lump formed in my throat as I watched my six-year-old shout "love you too" as he raced toward the building after his older sister. She was in a hurry to get to her friends. He was in a hurry to annoy her. Blessedly, thankfully, they both ran to join their classmates and teachers. Without fear. Without anxiety.

On Friday we talked about what happened. We talked about people that made bad choices. We talked about good and evil; about God and Satan. I asked questions about their school and the various drills they practice. They proudly told me about orange drills and fire drills and every other kind of drill. It reminded them how safe their school is. It reminded me, too.

We talked about guns. We talked about the guns in our locked safe, enclosed in a cabinet. Guns aren't bad. It seemed important for them to understand that bad people make bad choices. But we make good choices. We take care of our guns. We keep them safe. And, most importantly, we follow the law. I never want them to think people are bad because they own guns.

The unspoken question loomed, though. Why? There are easy answers (see also "excuses"), of course. He was ill. His parents divorced. He played violent video games. He had access to guns. He was socially awkward.

I don't believe in excuses. I don't believe humans can be defined quite that easily. I do believe in God. And I am defined by my faith in Him.

Why did God let this happen? Because we are humans. Because we constantly fail. We make messes. We judge. We bully. We lie and cheat and steal. We hate. Free will gives us the ability to make a choice. The great thing about free will is that last part. Choice. As easily as we make messes, we can clean them up; with our words and with our actions. We can help a friend. We can smile at a stranger. We can love. In spite of our human failings, we love.

Romans 12:21 says, "Do not be overcome by evil, but overcome evil with good." As surely as evil exists, good exists. And there is so much good. God gave us the will to choose the good.

Debates will continue. Sides will be chosen. New laws will be discussed. The conversations in the coming weeks will become contentious. I'll leave that to the experts.

Here, in our little house in a small town not much different than Newtown, we will pray. We will pray for goodness and for peace and for clarity. We will pray for the families. We will pray for the school.

And I will silently thank God that my children ran into their school today, feeling just as safe and secure as they did before Friday.

About the Author

Pauline is a proud stay-at-home wife and mother of three. By "at home" she means everywhere but home. She spends her time volunteering for various projects and charities as well as being "that mom" on the PTO and school board. After her family, she lives for coffee, football, and sharing her opinion with anyone that will (and sometimes won't) listen! She's an unabashed pro-life Catholic. Please follow her on Twitter at https://twitter.com/MiStateFan or visit clashdaily.com.

The fact that a gun may be black or have a military-style appearance doesn't make it any more dangerous than most of the rifles or shotguns used by American hunters on a daily basis.

FIREARMS 101: GUN INFORMATION FOR THE UNINFORMED

Written By R.G. Yoho

19 December 2012

Since the tragic shooting at the Connecticut elementary school, America has been subjected to a full-court press of lies, hysteria, and misinformation.

It's disturbing that the media, celebrities, and politicians are nearly gleeful about the deaths of this many children, an incident that might finally give them the excuse to ban guns in America.

In addition, a number of Americans get their information from programs like *The View*, which is littered with personalities like Whoopi Goldberg and Joy Behar, people who know absolutely nothing about guns, but arrogantly proclaim their views like they do.

Therefore, I have attempted to create a brief and overly-simplified lexicon on guns that you can share with the woefully uninformed. Perhaps it will help to correct the errors that have been, in many cases, deliberately perpetrated and perpetuated by politicians and the media.

Please understand that these definitions were NOT written for the informed gun owner; they were created for those citizens who believe every gang member in America has an UZI:

Automatic: This is a weapon that fires multiple bullets with a SINGLE trigger pull. Private citizens cannot own them without a special license. They are ALREADY illegal for the general public. Automatic weapons are almost exclusively held by the police and military. Moreover, they are ONLY prominently used on the streets of America in fictionalized, television and movie dramas.

Semiautomatic: This is a gun that fires only ONE shot for each individual trigger pull. They can be — and often are — used by sportsmen and hunters. Each trigger pull fires a shot, expels the empty cartridge, and chambers another round. They are no more dangerous than a revolver, or a firearm that expels a spent shell or cartridge by means of a lever, pump, or bolt action.

Assault Rifle: This is a term which has no clearly defined meaning. It was coined by those who know almost nothing about guns or how they actually operate. Journalists and politicians routinely use the term to create fear in the minds of the public, hoping to falsely create the notion that every Second Amendment enthusiast has a "machine gun." Quite often, the term is applied to guns that operate precisely like your average hunting rifle, routinely used to kill whitetail deer.

The fact that a gun may be black or have a military-style appearance doesn't make it any more dangerous than most of the rifles or shotguns used by American hunters on a daily basis.

Like any tool, guns can be misused and become dangerous when they are in the wrong hands. However, the tragic shootings that are committed by a few individuals with diseased and evil minds are only stopped by the introduction of other guns from the brave, decent, and honorable people who willingly choose to confront them.

And in some cases, that has been done by your neighbor down the street, the one who has a Concealed Carry permit.

By the way, if you hear somebody saying that the Founders never wanted you to practice your Second Amendment rights with a semiautomatic weapon, kindly ask them if they are exercising their First Amendment rights with a quill pen.

About the Author

Author R.G. Yoho is the author of three Westerns, including "Death Comes to Redhawk."

In addition to his Westerns, R.G. recently published a work of non-fiction, "America's History is His Story."

Please check out his Author's Page on Facebook: http://www.Facebook.com/R.G.Yoho

Had the principal of that school been gun savvy and had one with her none of this would have happened.

Reacting to Newtown: Tragedy and Rationality

Written By Suzanne Olden

19 December 2012

I started writing this article Friday afternoon. I had to stop because I was too upset. That was a good thing. What wasn't so good was the immediate presence of the "ban all guns" rhetoric and "kill all the NRA apologists" incendiary posts. Soon after were the gun right's supporter's responses.

It all bugged me, but not for the reasons you might think. Yes, I am a gun rights, Second Amendment supporter, and there were arguments made that I would get behind. What bugged me is that it started before the smoke had even cleared from the school hallways. For God's sake people, let the families have five minutes to mourn! That was not the time!

I would first like to condemn and place every ounce of responsibility squarely where it belongs, on the individual who thought it was perfectly ok to go into an elementary school and use children as targets. He, and only he, is responsible for this tragedy. Not gun owners, not the NRA, not the lack of mental health care, not Republicans, NO ONE BUT THE SHOOTER IS RESPONSIBLE FOR THIS ATTROCITY!

Had he not shot himself, he should have been caught, tried and held accountable for his actions. As it stands, he is facing more accountability than we can imagine. I'm not saying he is roasting in hell, what I am saying is he is standing before God, answering for his actions. What happens from there is up to God.

For this response to a Facebook friend's rant about how the lack of adequate mental health care is to blame, I was called "evil." Nice twist there, right? The shooter is sick, not evil, but someone who says he should be held accountable is evil. Wow!

I posted on my social media that everyone from gun control advocates to gun rights advocates should be respectful to those affected directly by this tragedy and to respectfully wait to debate the issues. The responses I got were varied but ran the gamut from agreeing with me, to saying that everyone deals differently and let them vent, to the most unbelievably hateful. Several gun control advocates gave me the "if not now, when" argument.

I'll give one friend credit, after I called him out about politicizing it, we chatted offline and he told me he didn't agree with me, but he could see my point. He said he was "one angry parent" which plays right into my position. How can you have any kind of meaningful debate or dialogue with anyone when they are angry and emotional?

The rest of the responses were along the lines of one Twitter user who said "how dare you use the word respect and still agree with the USA current gun laws after what's happened?"

I dare. Owning a gun or supporting the right to do so doesn't make me disrespectful of anyone.

Another started with ""I call bulls**t on that!! Wait a few days!! Idiot NRA apologists!" Apologist? I've never apologized for the NRA. After I responded to him with "so wrong on so many levels" and "does calling names make you feel better? It certainly shows me you're capable of cogent discussion…" he tweeted these final two: "many levels? Wow, how sharp you must be. Maybe Santa will bring you a brain this year or at least one that functions."

See, I'm stupid because I disagree with him. Wonder if he knows what cogent means. Then he continued his diatribe with "maybe out of respect for the families the GUNMAN should have just killed himself!!!! And a few NRA idiots!" Ok, so you're against gun violence unless people disagree with you, then you're all for shooting them. Confused much? I blocked him after that. Life's too short.

My only two cents beyond the above is this: Had the principal of that school been gun savvy and had one with her none of this would have happened. Here's why. *The Today Show* on Monday morning had a report that said this: "He shoots at a school window and shatters it to get in. At the sound of gunfire, Principal Dawn Hochsprung and school psychologist Mary Sherlach come running. They are immediately killed. ~~Name Deleted~~ then turns towards the Kindergarten classroom…"

Had the principal had a weapon and used it, game over. Kids live and one very bad man is stopped. Can we sort out later that the shooter had mental illness issues? Sure. Can we discuss assault weapons and their availability? Sure. Would we have had the above scenario happen? Nope. In fact, the principal probably would have been demonized for having a gun on a school campus. We know now she would have saved the lives of twenty-six people and twenty children. Still wouldn't have mattered to the gun control crowd.

I'll end with this. My brother, a minister, wrote an eloquent post about how people react to tragedies such as this by assigning blame. He said, and I agree, that we need to place blame to make sense of the senseless. My pleas to wait to do so were not received well because of this, and I can see that. What I don't think is ok is the hatefulness that came from some people. That is never ok. So let's debate and discuss, but do it with respect for each other. The rest will all sort itself out.

ABOUT THE AUTHOR

Suzanne Reisig Olden is a Catholic Christian, Conservative, married mother of two. She lives northwest of Baltimore, in Carroll County, Maryland. She graduated of Villa Julie College/Stevenson University with a BS in Paralegal Studies and works as a paralegal for a franchise company, specializing in franchise law and intellectual property. Originally from Baltimore, and after many moves, she came home to raise her son and daughter, now ages 17 and 13, in her home state. Suzanne also writes for the online publication, *The Beacon Bulletin*.

Read more of her work at http://beaconbulletin.com/.

Then, in my research, I made a frightening discovery. The Japanese bathtub is more dangerous than the American handgun. Julian Ryall, correspondent for the UK TELE-GRAPH, reported from Tokyo in April of this year, that "Japan's health ministry is to launch an investigation into bath-time fatalities after it was estimated that 14,000 people die every year in the tub – three times as many as those who died in car accidents."

A "GOOD CRISIS": PRESIDENT OBAMA CRASHES A FUNERAL

Written By John Kirkwood

20 December 2012

The first thing that I noticed was how cool the revolver looked. I'm not a type of guy who "blings" out his handguns, but a piece painted to look like the American flag would look nice in a shadowbox over my pulpit. Then I made the mistake of reading the words. The poster was part of a HANDGUN CONTROL INC. propaganda drive from 1981. It read, "Last year, handguns killed 48 people in Japan; 8 in Great Britain; 34 in Switzerland; 52 in Canada; 58 in Israel; 21 in Sweden; 42 in West Germany; 10,728 in the United States. God Bless America."

In her rush to show her compassion and enlightenment, the NPR ditz that posted it didn't bother to check the figures or the date and didn't mind looking like a crass grouse for posting it on her "pro Second Amendment" friend's Facebook wall. Before the children of Sandy Hook were even laid to rest, this liberal along with dozens of democrats and reporters were pining for gun bans. How many mini-"Wellstone memorials" have you had to endure since the Newtown shooting spree? It appears that liberal hearts no longer bleed; they spew.

For the sake of argument, let's not get bogged down with the figures because they probably haven't changed much. Let's not even sweat the fact that the mouth-breather who penned the ad can't tell the difference between a hunk of metal incapable of carrying out a homicide and the criminals (not mentioned) that can. Let's simply think about those numbers for a second.

If you really want to do a side-by-side comparison of numbers, you want to make sure that you adjust for population and make sure that the variables are similar so the distinction is apparent. Comparing a country with 350 million people, 90 million gun owners and 300 million firearms to a country with 10 million sheeple and full frontal gun restrictions, isn't the height of statistical analysis. Last I checked; Sweden's urban areas weren't over run with Bloods and Crips "negotiating" distribution rights.

To make this comparison is as foolish as comparing the number of traffic accidents that women drivers cause in America to that of Saudi Arabia. Judging solely on the numbers, you'd have to believe that American women should be stripped of their driver's licenses. There are even some American women, known as "traffic stoppers", who cause accidents even when they're not behind the wheel. If the warden's wife from *Cool Hand Luke* is washing the car in the drive, there is a high probability that there will be at least one fender bender and possibly a couple of domestic disturbances. So while you're taking the ladies drivers licenses, better make sure that Kate Upton et al is all "burka'd up."

Excuse for the moment that Columbia and Thailand have doubled our homicide rate with "handguns" and South Africa tripled; but the poster had me so worked up that I started to look up the national figures for "number of fatalities" in automobile accidents. America led the way there too, and the numbers were even wider.

Of course we have more cars and more drivers than anyone else in the world and our cars are a bit more buff than the rider mowers that you find in euro-land. But where exactly is the hue and cry from the politicians over our highway mortality rate? Three and sometimes four times as many Americans are killed in or by automobiles then they are by "firearms" and not one politician will dare to suppress our driving "rights."

As I write this, not one major American figure in politics or journalism has asked for a national dialogue on mental illness or the ACLU's role in relaxing the institutionalizing of "bat crap crazies." Maybe it's just me, but if The Sandy Hook Shooter flew over the cuckoo's nest, I'd be all for Nurse Ratched lighting him up with a Remington 870.

Then, in my research, I made a frightening discovery. The Japanese bathtub is more dangerous than the American handgun. Julian Ryall, correspondent for the UK TELEGRAPH, reported from Tokyo in April of this year, that "Japan's health ministry is to launch an investigation into bath-time fatalities after it was estimated that 14,000 people die every year in the tub – three times as many as those who died in car accidents."

Incredible! To be consistent I think it would be prudent to call for registration and licensing of all Japanese bathtubs. The SEIU should give classes in how to bathe safely and Planned Parenthood should distribute pamphlets instructing the young and the old about the crisis. Until one passes the course, they should simply not be allowed to bathe alone; the sponge bath and wet wipes can cover in the interim. Bob Costas should come out with an impassioned monologue about the Japanese Bath Culture and ask that we must all commit to stopping random acts of hygiene. (Occupy Wall Street is already on board.) We should also reconsider the amendment that makes bathing a constitutionally protected right – in light of the carnage, we can't be bound to the antiquated.

A few hours later, a friend shared a poster to my wall. This one showed FBI and CDC statistics that put "firearm homicides" as the 10th "biggest killer" in the United States (11, 493), trailing Tobacco Use (529,000) and Medical Errors (195,000), along with seven other components including Non Firearm Homicides (16,799). It has a caption at the bottom that says, "According to the FBI, the #1 weapon used in violent crimes is the baseball bat."

Although I do believe this poster is more consistently accurate than the first poster, it contains a crucial error. While the chart makes a good point, it's interesting to note what was left out. The biggest killer in the United States is not tobacco, not by a long shot. The biggest killer in America is abortion. Mothers in America choose about 1.4 million times a year to kill their own sons and daughters. So no, I guess the baseball bat isn't the preferred weapon for violent crime; it's the scalpel.

Just days after the mass shooting in Newtown Connecticut where a mentally deranged man murdered 26 people, 20 of them elementary age children; President Obama went on the air to politicize the event. As a pre-cursor to an unprecedented gun grab, the man who voted on four different occasions to "shelve" babies born of a botched abortion asked, "Can we say that we are truly doing enough, to give all of the children of this country the chance they deserve to live out their lives in happiness and with purpose?"

I've just got to ask, Mr. President; do your words apply to the children in the womb as well? Do they apply to the children that you voted to put on a shelf until they "expired?"

Does it sicken you that the president, with our mayors and representatives, and the "watchdogs" in the media, are so eager to exploit the death of 20 innocent children; so willing to go "on script" with their inane solutions even before the casings hit the floor? Yet for forty years, some 28,000 children are "killed" every week and there is nothing but silence from our shepherds.

The irony in that number is that Newtown, Connecticut's population is just shy of 28,000 people. Now imagine walking into Newtown every week and finding every man, woman and child murdered. How would the media report that? What would be the outrage if they didn't? Why hasn't the President preempted a football game for a tragedy of that magnitude? Why haven't the mayors of major cities called for legislation? Why isn't Bob Costas bemoaning America's abortion culture? Why aren't our artists coming together to hold concerts for the victims? Who is holding a moment of silence for the victims of the hidden holocaust?

Yet, the president has the stones to quote the God of the Bible, and we have the arrogance to ask "Where was God?" Where's God? It's not like we don't know He's there. We know it and we're content to turn the shoulder and flip Him off. We haven't forgotten God; we've forsaken Him.

If each of the 54 million babies that have died in the forty years since Roe v Wade had their own moment of silence, it would last for over 100 years. So next time we wonder "where was God" in a moment of national tragedy – well maybe He's just observing that moment of silence.

About the Author

John Kirkwood is a son of Issachar. He is a Zionist, gun-toting, cigar-smoking, incandescent light bulb-using, 3.2 gallon flushing, fur-wearing, Chinese (MSG) eating, bow-hunting, SUV driving, unhyphenated American man who loves his wife, isn't ashamed of his country and does not apologize for his Christianity. He Pastors Grace Gospel Fellowship Bensenville, where "we the people" seek to honor "In God we Trust." He hosts the Christian wake up call IN THE ARENA every Sunday at noon on AM 1160 and he co-hosts Un-Common Sense, the Christian Worldview with a double shot of espresso on UncommonShow.com. He is the proud homeschooling dad of Konnor, Karter and Payton and the "blessed from heaven above" husband of the Righteous and Rowdy Wendymae.

We used to be a society populated by people who attended services weekly at least. In those services they heard about the God of love. They also heard about the wages of sin, his wrath being poured out on evil, the joys of heaven, and the perils of hell. They learned the value of inspired virtue, and they learned to fear the One who could throw them into hell.

Newtown, CT Massacre – Broken Hearts, Broken Minds, Broken Lives

Written by Allan Erickson

20 December 2012

> Many kinds of broken hearts,
>
> All deep searing pain,
>
> Yet none so devastating as seeing
>
> The innocent slain.

Another atrocity, this one worse than any before. Little kids. And a good deal more little ones dispatched since 1973, ones who never made it to school.

In the end it doesn't matter if the shooter was mentally ill. It doesn't matter if he bought the guns or stole them. It doesn't matter if gun control laws in Connecticut are sufficient.

The problem is not external and therefore the solution is not external. The problem does not reside outside the walls of the home, outside the walls of the school, or outside the halls of legislatures.

The problem is not without: it is within.

We read not so long ago about a pastor in Texas beaten to death by a man wielding an electric guitar.

A couple weeks back, in Ohio, a man beat his wife to death with a banjo.

Did anyone circulate a petition to ban stringed instruments?

The problem is not external and therefore the solution is not external. Well-meaning road-to-hell "progressives" can march on the NRA and the mayor of New York can demand the President confiscate every gun in the world. It won't matter.

And it doesn't really matter if the shooter was sane or insane or partially sane or flat-out evil. A killer is a killer, and people died, even little kids.

What matters is agreeing on the best way to encourage good behavior by the majority, and the best way to prevent bad behavior in the very few. Laws only go so far to discourage bad behavior. Peer pressure can only do so much in stifling the bad and promoting the good.

The human heart is the problem.

We used to be a society populated by people who attended services weekly at least. In those services they heard about the God of love. They also heard about the wages of sin, his wrath being poured out on evil, the joys of heaven, and the perils of hell. They learned the value of inspired virtue, and they learned to fear the One who could throw them into hell.

Were there atrocities then? Of course: but they were fewer and farther between, and when they happened, people fell on their knees in repentance. It is clear: we are better off when leather-lunged preachers outnumber the psychologists.

Yet, today, we continue to shake our fists at God, and demand more laws and more shrinks and more medication.

We reject the heart surgeon and call on the bureaucrat and the pharmacist.

Our poisonous permissiveness encourages violence in media, allowing children to play the most violent video games, giving them license to watch and listen to the most vile things, thinking those sights and sounds inconsequential. Every time the consequences explode in another blood bath, the best we can do is step up the verbal violence invoking the blame game, and demand more laws, calling ourselves wise.

Never mind the tightest gun laws coexist in areas with the highest gun violence.

Our only hope is in a virtuous citizenry volunteering to do right by one another. No such citizenry exists apart from the power of the God of Love.

Our only consolation: knowing God's justice will ultimately prevail, that the innocents slain have a special place in His paradise.

And, the moment we ask him to make us a virtuous people, he begins the transformation.

In the meanwhile, we insist on stubborn self-reliance, and therefore, evil is emboldened and atrocities flourish.

About the Author

Allan Erickson enjoyed an 11-year career in radio, television and print journalism as a reporter, talk show host, and operations manager. He then turned to sales and marketing for a decade. Ten years ago he started his own training and recruitment company in the Pacific Northwest. Allan & wife Jodi have four children and live in California. He is also the author of "*The Cross & the Constitution in the Age of Incoherence,*" Tate Publishing, 2012.

If there are three provable reported instances of agreed upon signs of dangerous or threatening psychotic behavior that individual is removed from the premises. He would then be taken for treatment by the local mental health authorities.

Mental Illness was True Triggerman — Not Lax Gun Control Laws

Written By Kevin Fobbs

20 December 2012

There was a fear moving across the American heartland long before ~~Name Deleted~~ stepped onto the nation's stage and donned the dark murderous mass killer robe. This twenty-year-old joined the unique club of notable mass murderers that used a gun as a weapon of slaughter. After his onslaught the hysteria surrounding stricter gun control legislation has risen to an emotional fever pitch. But is this response the rational or correct conclusion that is the definitive answer to this gunman's deadly outburst?

This rapid rush to judgment and instant condemnation of guns as the casual factor for the mindless killings by a disturbed gunman is just too convenient a straw man. The mainstream media, along with the urgency of the gun control first responders keep overlooking the obvious. Disturbed gunmen have used a legal weapon, when it is their very mental illness that is the true deadly assault weapon!

The loss of such precious young children, teachers and the murderer's mother Nancy should not be buried in the grave with the actual culprit to their senseless murders. The Sandy Hook killer, a mentally disturbed young man, stole three legally registered weapons to commit his crimes; the emphasis is on legal. The actual crimes were formulated in his head and his conduct, unrestrained by possible intervention of law enforcement or mental health authorities, became the deadly weapon.

So why do politicians want to dismember the constitutional right to arm to protect the life of an individual or a family or to use for legitimate purpose, defined by the individual and not by government?

These officials are afraid to tackle the hard question and solution to this outrage. They absolutely refuse to hold the individual who had a mental illness, and had shown previous signs, and crossed the line into forceful dangerous behavior, responsible for his actions.

Instead, this tragic cat and mouse game is played on the national stage by congress, state legislatures, and mayors like Michael Bloomberg who hide behind their own protective guards and trained security. They find it quite easy to take a steamroller over the U.S. Constitution's Second Amendment. This endless tag game will eventually die down as the holidays, the New Year and another fiscal cliff crisis takes on the headlines.

But in far too many homes in America, there are tens of thousands of families who hide in their bedrooms, or in their kitchen or basement praying that someone in law enforcement or the mental health community will intervene. They wish someone could help restrain, or intervene when their mentally challenged child, or young adult continues to threaten, continues to be abusive until he takes the possible next step toward unrestrained violence.

But liberals do not want to have that national discussion, because they would rather point the finger at gun owners, because that is easy. Yet this mother or father or sibling, or even neighbor needs a solution that will last past today's headlines.

To keep the next Aurora, Colorado, or New Town, Conn from becoming the new tragedy, a "Three Strike Rule" to help identify and remove a potentially violent mentally unstable person from the home must be seriously considered. If there are three provable reported instances of agreed upon signs of dangerous or threatening psychotic behavior that individual is removed from the premises. He would then be taken for treatment by the local mental health authorities.

The individual who perpetrates the criminal act should be the legitimate focus, not the weapon he used. When this type of behavior is identified and the person removed before murdering family members and other innocents, then the family is protected and the community is safeguarded against this potentially dangerous individual.

According to Fox News, "A senior law enforcement official involved in the investigation confirmed that ~~Name Deleted~~ was angry over his mother's possible plans for his "future mental health treatment." Officials have speculated that his anger was a possible motive for the deadly tragic assaults. If either the murderer's mother or law enforcement had access to a "Three Strike Rule" removal process, her deranged son would have been taken before the attacks and her murder.

The nation must take a step back from this frenzied behavior to not emotionally lose objectivity when a tragedy pains the nation as this has done. America does need answers, but they will not be found in the legal books of Connecticut or Colorado because they have strict gun laws, and these mass murders were not averted. A "Three Strike Rule" is a workable solution which can be used to prevent another unbalanced gunman from causing more tragedies.

ABOUT THE AUTHOR

Kevin Fobbs has more than 35 years of wide-ranging experience as a community and tenant organizer, Legal Services outreach program director, public relations consultant, business executive, gubernatorial and presidential appointee, political advisor, widely published writer, and national lecturer. Kevin is co-chair and co-founder of AC-3 (American-Canadian Conservative Coalition) that focuses on issues on both sides of the border between the two countries.

I have a six-year-old son, and I thought of him that morning. The thought of all those first graders dying almost made me vomit. I had to fight back the bile in my throat all day long, and I ate very little food that day.

Michigan Gov Doesn't Understand: the Wolf is at the Door and He Wants Our Guns!

<u>Written By Skip Coryell</u>

20 December 2012

The other day I was taking a walk down a country road when I came across the strangest sight. I saw two timber wolves creeping up on a flock of sheep in a farmer's pen. The wolves were pretty big and shaggy, and they bared their teeth and snarled as they got closer. I could actually see the saliva dripping off their fangs. It was an awesome sight, and I remember thinking "Wow! How many people actually get to see a wolf take down its prey in real life?"

But then the weirdest thing happened. Just as the wolves were about to pounce and rip the sheep to shreds, the scrawniest sheep of the flock stepped forward and raised up a sign that said "No Wolves Allowed".

The larger of the two wolves stood up from his crouch, and I heard him say, "Damn it, Joe, that's the third sign we've seen this week!" And both the wolves slouched away in angry compliance.

Hmmm, does anyone believe that story? Well, unfortunately, the answer is yes. Lots of people. In fact, they believe it so much they place their lives and the lives of their children in the hands of a sign everyday when they send their children to school.

I write this because something similar just happened here in my home state of Michigan. Governor Rick Snyder just vetoed Senate bill 59, legislation that would allow concealed carry holders with advanced training to carry concealed in schools, day care centers, churches, and other places where most mass shootings occur. Apparently he vetoed the bill for the safety and well being of the children.

Question: What is the best way to stop a bad guy with a gun?

Answer: Have a good guy shoot him.

A study of mass shootings over the past two decades tells us two things:

1. You can't stop a lunatic from killing. He'll find a way.

2. He'll kill as many as he can until he's met with armed resistance. Then he'll kill himself.

In light of that, doesn't it make sense to kill the lunatic as quickly as possible? But you say, "Skip, that is so callous, so cold. How can you talk that way? Simple. My very first thought when I heard the report on the Sandy Hook school shootings was this: "I wish I had been there to kill the deranged murderer."

I don't say that because I'm blood thirsty. I say that because I love children and they deserve to live. Mass murderers deserve to die.

I have a six-year-old son, and I thought of him that morning. The thought of all those first graders dying almost made me vomit. I had to fight back the bile in my throat all day long, and I ate very little food that day.

And now, just when safety for Michigan's children was in sight, Governor Rick Snyder did the one thing that guarantees these mass shootings will continue. He vetoed the bill that would have saved our kids. Is he cold? No. Is he heartless? No. Is he stupid? No. In fact, I've heard he's a really nice guy. But the problem with Governor Snyder is this: He's a sheep.

He means well, but he's just not qualified to protect the flock. He doesn't have the temperament or the courage or the warrior mindset to do the right thing. A few hours after the veto I got an email from the Rick Snyder Defense Fund spear-headed by One Nation PAC. They are anticipating the big Unions will try to take out Snyder like they did Governor Walker in Wisconsin. (Snyder just signed the Right to Work bill into law.)

I remember supporting Governor Walker with letters and emails. I even donated money for his defense. But I won't be doing that for Governor Snyder. I'll be damned if I'll help protect a grown man who doesn't have the courage and decency to protect small children in school.

Governor Snyder is a sheep, and I'm inclined to let the Union have their pound of wool.

ABOUT THE AUTHOR

Skip Coryell lives with his wife and children in Michigan. Skip Coryell is the author of nine books including *Blood in the Streets: Concealed Carry and the OK Corral*, *RKBA: Defending the Right to Keep and Bear Arms*, *The God Virus*, and *We Hold These Truths*. He is the founder of The Second Amendment March, a Marine Corps veteran, and the President of White Feather Press. He is an avid hunter and sportsman, a Marine Corps veteran, and a graduate of Cornerstone University. For more details on Skip Coryell, or to contact him personally, go to his web-site at skipcoryell.com

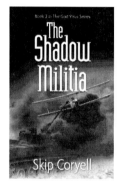

To get a copy of Skip's latest novel *The Shadow Militia*, go to store.whitefeather-press.com or amazon.com.

Look, if my kid was walking around with goth crap on and a Moe Howard haircut, carrying a black briefcase to class and enjoying pulling the legs off live frogs, I wouldn't take my little Lee Harvey to the gun range.

Massacre Prevention Alert: Ban High Capacity Idiots, Not High Capacity Magazines

Written By Doug Giles

20 December 2012

The composite of Satan's spawn, (name of murderer deleted by publisher), is starting to unfurl, and unfortunately we are forced to learn more and more about this murderous grunt.

Reports from family friends, relatives and schoolmates describe the murderer as, "intelligent, but unloving and anti-social." By the looks of some of his Manson-like school pics, Stevie Wonder could've seen that this toad was channeling some major voodoo.

My question for the deceased mother is, "Why the heck would you teach this demoniac how to shoot? Your kid was seriously jacked up, and your answer was let's get him into guns?" Whiskey Tango Foxtrot, lady. Eternal hindsight's 20/20, eh?

Hey, Mom, why didn't you get your scary child into Nerf balls, or Frisbee Golf or Badminton? Or if he wanted to remain the loner you should have gotten him into frickin' Hacky Sack.

Yep, if you weren't going to discipline that little Damien you should have at least gotten him on medical marijuana—I'm talking the most potent skunk weed known to mankind—and pushed him toward games with soft objects not guns and Call of Duty. Geez, lady … what were you thinking? Oh, and dad … where were you?

Look, if my kid was walking around with goth crap on and a Moe Howard haircut, carrying a black briefcase to class and enjoying pulling the legs off live frogs, I wouldn't take my little Lee Harvey to the gun range.

No, instead I would try to discipline that smack out of him. I'm talkin' old school West Texas style. In addition, I would make sure everywhere T-Rex went that he was surrounded by elevator music and paintings of sweet bunny rabbits. And I sure as shizzle wouldn't have any guns or sharp objects around him.

If this formula of discipline and a relaxed environment didn't cure him after 16 years then I'd send him to Shady Acres Looney Bin and have them scrape his frontal lobe. But that's just me.

Mom … dad … if you have a ticking bomb in your house and you own guns, do us all a favor and get a gun safe, have the key surgically implanted into your colon, and only go hunting and shooting when your "special" boy is away from the house at electroshock therapy or having his weekly exorcism. It could save a lot of lives…

About Doug Giles

Doug Giles is the man behind ClashDaily.com. In addition to driving ClashDaily.com, Giles is a popular columnist on Townhall.com and the author of the book Raising Righteous & Rowdy Girls.

Doug's articles have also appeared on several other print and online news sources, including The Washington Times, The Daily Caller, Fox Nation, USA Today, The Wall Street Journal, The Washington Examiner, The Blaze, American Hunter Magazine and ABC News.

He's been a frequent guest on the Fox News Channel and Fox Business Channel as well as many nationally syndicated radio shows across the nation — which, he believes, officially makes him a super hero.

In addition, Doug is an occasional guest host on New York City's WABC (The Jason Mattera Show) and he is a weekly guest, every Friday at 7:45am[et], on America's Morning News (155 markets).

Giles and his wife Margaret have two daughters: Hannah, who devastated ACORN with her 2009 nation shaking undercover videos, and Regis who is an NRA columnist, huntress and Second Amendment activist.

DG's interests include guns, big game hunting, big game fishing, fine art, cigars, helping wounded warriors, and being a big pain in the butt to people who dislike God and the USA.

Read more Doug Giles at www.clashdaily.com.

In the United States, we do not do things for the "benefit" of the state. If we did things for the benefit of the state, then we would have no First Amendment, Fourth Amendment, or Fifth Amendment—or any of the others, for that matter. In the Founders' view, the state exists only to prevent injustice (see: Locke, John, and Bastiat, Frederic for further clarification).

GUN-RIGHTS Q & A WITH A LIBERAL

Written by Michell Zook

21 December 2012

Q: Shouldn't we ban assault weapons?

A: All weapons are "assault" weapons and almost anything can be a weapon. By this statement, I take it that you're in favor of banning high-heeled shoes, pillows, knives, guns, hockey sticks, baseball bats, coasters, automobiles, tools, furniture, some varieties of plants, laundry detergent, wasp spray, wine bottles, etc…

Q: Okay, well, why not just assault rifles?

A: There is no such thing as an assault rifle. Guns come in two varieties: automatic and semi-automatic. You can read here where Dana Loesch schools libs on the differences, and since most people here know guns, I won't bore you with an extensive definition.

Q: But do you really need a high-capacity magazine or a shotgun with a pistol grip?

A: I don't know, do you really "need" a car? Do you really "need" a boat? Cars kill a lot more people than guns, and you have no Constitutional right to own a car.

Q: But how can you claim you have a Constitutional right to own a high-capacity magazine?

A: How can you claim I don't? The Second Amendment is very clear. It says, *"A well regulated militia, being necessary to the security of a free state, the right of the people to keep and bear arms, shall not be infringed."* That means my right to keep and bear guns (and the munitions to employ said guns) shall not be infringed upon by the state. If I want a high-capacity magazine (and the gun to go with it), then the state should not be able to prevent me from owning one.

Q: In the Founders' time, they only had muskets. They couldn't conceive of a time when people would want such things or surely they would have prohibited it, right?

A: They also couldn't have conceived of a right to an abortion, taxpayer-funded healthcare or a welfare state, but I am assured that those things are covered by the Constitution. Shall we rethink our positions on those?

Q: But providing for the poor benefits the state. Guns don't benefit the state, so how can we justify still maintaining them?

A: In the United States, we do not do things for the "benefit" of the state. If we did things for the benefit of the state, then we would have no First Amendment, Fourth Amendment, or Fifth Amendment—or any of the others, for that matter. In the Founders' view, the state exists only to prevent injustice (see: Locke, John, and Bastiat, Frederic for further clarification).

Q: So you think everyone in the country should run around with guns?

A: Only if they're comfortable carrying one (I don't think it should be forced or coercive) and I would hope people would be responsible about it. While I don't think I should have to get a license when it's time for my little ones to start out with their .22s, I also think the idea of concealed carry classes is a good one, if only to explain the laws and ensure people are comfortable and responsible with firearms.

Q: What about teachers?

A: I think if teachers have concealed carry licenses and want to carry them, they should be free to carry them, with stipulations that the principal is aware of it and that they are required to maintain the firearm on their person and not in a purse or a drawer accessible to students. Gun free zones haven't worked out so well. Let's even the playing field a little.

Q: What if there's a crazy teacher?

A: If someone is too irresponsible to be trusted with the safety of students, they should not be teaching. Period.

Q: What if they go crazy while they're teaching and they realize they have access to a weapon?

A: While we're dealing with hypotheticals, perhaps you've never seen the damage a crazed teacher could do with a stapler, a pair of scissors, or even just a desk chair.

Q: But don't you think criminals shouldn't have access to guns?

A: Don't you think they already do? Shouldn't I be able to defend myself and my family from them?

Q: But if guns are accessible, then people can use them to murder others, right?

A: And if alcohol is accessible, then alcoholics can use it to get drunk and then they might murder someone with their car. If we restrict guns, then people (crazy people included) will resort to other ways of murdering. Cain certainly didn't need a gun to murder Abel!

Q: Fair enough. But this still doesn't explain why anyone would need a high-capacity magazine or a pistol grip on a shotgun, so why can't we ban those?

A: Why can't we ban V-8 engines or luxury cars? Please explain to me why those are necessary. Furthermore, the Second Amendment is the ultimate protection against tyranny. What do you think the police or military would employ if they needed to subdue an area of the country?

Q: So you think people should own bazookas or (other military grade weapon)?

A: Why not? If they can afford it and possess the know-how to operate it, then who are you to prohibit them from having it? Personally, I would prefer a Tavor.

ABOUT THE AUTHOR

A native Texan currently living it up in Utah, Michelle served five years in the Air Force as an Air Battle Manager, attaining the rank of captain. These days, she's pursuing a MA Public Policy at Liberty University, learning the ropes as a military spouse, chasing two little ones around, staying caught up on the news, and trying not to meddle in her husband's career. She's a firm believer in states' rights, the Second Amendment and individual liberties.

If your child, friend, or spouse is playing violent video games that are titled "Kindergarten Killer" it's time you intervened.

SHOCK ALERT: Kindergarten Killer Videogame

Written by Regis Giles

21 December 2012

Wayne LaPierre referenced in his speech today, as he addressed the Connecticut school shootings, that there is a video game out there titled "*Kindergarten Killer*". Curious, I went looking for it and it turns out it does exist. And it's free!

Here is the description of the game:

> "*As a hitman for hire, you were recently given orders to take out the headmaster of a kindergarten school. Your job is to not ask questions, so you carry on with the job and head to the school. One thing leads to the next and you accidentally kill a teacher. The kids saw it and they get riled up. The children rise up in arms and open fire at you at every chance they get. But despite everything that happened, your target still roams alive so you head back to the office and kill your target before heading back to the office. Enjoy a crazy shootout in Kindergarten Killer.*"

Who is the messed up soul that created this game? Honestly, our society has dropped to new lows. I wouldn't be surprised if jack-wagon L--za played this game often and took notes.

Ladies and gents, we as a society need to wake up and pay attention. If your child, friend, or spouse is playing violent video games that are titled "*Kindergarten Killer*" it's time you intervened. Take that person out to lunch, for a hike, fishing… anything that will get them away from the computer and TV, from that digitized world of killing and bring them back to reality.

If it takes a village to raise a child, then it's going to take a nation to prevent the next school massacre.

About the Author

Regis Giles is the creator and owner of GirlsJustWannaHaveGuns.com and is a leading voice for Second Amendment rights, self-defense and conservationism. Unafraid to speak her mind, Regis takes no prisoners. Her media appearances include: ELLE Magazine, The Daily Mail, ABC, CNN, & Fox News.

Guns are not the problem. The human heart is the problem. Human insistence on proceeding apart from the God of love is the problem. The world view and life philosophy of people like Michael the Hut are the problem.

Jabba the Moore: Hammerhead Forever

Written by Allan Erickson

22 December 2012

Michael Moore shares his wisdom at Big Hollywood in the wake of the Sandy Hook tragedy: "I hate to say it, but killing is our way. We began America w/ genocide, then built it w/ slaves. The shootings will continue — it's who we are," Moore tweeted this weekend. [It is hateful to say it.]

"A country that officially sanctions horrific violence (invade Iraq, drones kill kids, death penalty) is surprised when a 20-yr old joins in?" [Yes, who needs rule of law, Acts of Congress, law and order, or just war theory? It's all the same.]

"It's all violence & it's all connected. Why does this happen only in America? The answer is right in front of u. And it's not just the guns." [Only in America? Just look for the union label.]

"The NRA hates freedom. They don't want you to have the freedom to send your children to school & expect them to come home alive." [One of the most reprehensible statements yet.]

Very comforting to the families, Mr. Moore.

Remember, this is the same genius who wanted us to believe Columbine was the fault of the NRA and the "military industrial complex," a term coined by President Eisenhower, someone who knew a few things about the value of the Second Amendment in the effort to derail tyrants. We learned later the boys who murdered their fellow students in Colorado were marinated in hate and violence thanks in large part to drugs and violent video games, things Moore never has condemned. Note that Michael spilled no tears for the Christian kids murdered that day.

In former days, before the nation drugged itself into a purple haze, a hammerhead like Michael Moore would have been ignored, or deported. The truly disturbing reality: millions of people agree with this intellectual slob.

Responses are in order, not that Jabba the Moore will ever learn or grow. It is hoped however that a few of his disciples will reconsider and contrast his fantasy world with truth and reason.

Genocide? Does he mean the tragic deaths of Native Americans by the accidental transmission of European diseases? If so, that's not genocide. Genocide is a collective national strategy to purposefully eradicate an entire people group. That is not what happened in America, despite what the revisionists would have you believe. As a great start toward a real education I'd recommend *Ten Biggest Lies about America*, by Michael Medved, a bonafide intellectual.

Killing is no more the American way exclusively than it is the Zambian or the Canadian way. Humans in all places in all times have done terrible things. Trying to single out America as the worst example is sheer propaganda driven by lies, Jabba's cinematic specialty. The truth is man is fallen, filled with sin, and prone to atrocity, separated as he is from his Creator, the God of love. Jabba will never acknowledge that truth, and therefore he places himself in the place of eternal error.

Jabba's communist friends have been responsible for the most "productive" genocidal lunacy in history. Tens of millions of men, women and children have been slaughtered in the name of enlightened communism since Karl Marx penned his manifesto. Today, Jabba promotes the same thinking that results in continuous genocide, ignores that reality, and fingers America, the only country consistently at the forefront of stopping genocide and the thugs who perpetrate it.

Only in America?

Jabba ignores the Chechnya school massacre at Beslan in 2004. Muslim terrorists killed 150 kids and 150 adults after terrorizing them for days. I guess that was just the Chechen way? Let's face it: Jabba has tunnel vision narrowed to the diameter of a drinking straw.

There are thousands upon thousands of other examples from across the waves. How many kids did the clerics in Tehran march into the guns and the gas behind Saddam's sadistic Stalinist vision. Does Jabba forget the massacre of youth in enlightened Norway not long ago, or the daily mutilation of little girls in the Islamic world? You get the picture.

Slavery? The truth is slavery was much more widespread in central and south America than in the U.S., and Europeans and Muslims worldwide were vastly more proficient in securing and transporting slaves, with the help of many Africans, by the way. To say that Americans were somehow the worst of the traders is ridiculous, and to claim slaves were mostly responsible for building the country? Idiotic. As if the tiny minority did all the work. Did they contribute beyond their numbers against their will? Of course. Was it a national shame and a sin? Of course. Did they build the entire country? Think it through for a moment or two and see the light.

Also, has anyone ever heard Jabba decry contemporary human trafficking, or the massive slave trade engaged by Muslims from North Africa east all the way through Indonesia? Of course not. Real slavers Jabba ignores. Like so many in the country, he can't stand seeing the civil rights movement progress in the wake of 600,000 dead during the Civil War. He'd rather pick at the wound and make it bleed.

After all, there's no political leverage in helping realize racial reconciliation.

As to "horrific violence," aside from the verbal violence encouraging physical violence thanks to Jabba the Thug, apparently he cannot differentiate between just war and criminal law.

As to drones, Jabba should take that up with Barry, his lord and savior.

The NRA hates freedom? That's like saying George Washington and Thomas Jefferson hate freedom. Both endorsed the Second Amendment, and if they were living today, they'd be card-carrying NRA members.

The fact is Jabba and meatheads like him are the true anti-liberty forces in this nation. They promote stifling tyranny in the name of their state-sponsored religion, secular humanism. They enslave people and economies with the organized crime of labor unions. They endorse the murder of unborn babies, then blame child shootings by a maniac on political opponents.

They cheapen life everyday by dismissing any life they warrant inconvenient or non-productive, then act morally outraged when the cheapening promotes heartlessness. Complete hypocrites.

In truth, anti-God forces lead by people like Jabba are responsible for the continual demoralization of the culture, the permissive society that promotes violence in Hollywood and in mockumentaries, and feral adolescents hypnotized by video games so violent they destroy conscience.

Sandy Hook Massacre

Guns are not the problem. The human heart is the problem. Human insistence on proceeding apart from the God of love is the problem. The world view and life philosophy of people like Michael the Hut are the problem.

If anyone is to blame for Sandy Hook, it's people like Jabba the Schlub.

ABOUT THE AUTHOR

Allan Erickson enjoyed an 11-year career in radio, television and print journalism as a reporter, talk show host, and operations manager. He then turned to sales and marketing for a decade. Ten years ago he started his own training and recruitment company in the Pacific Northwest. Allan & wife Jodi have four children and live in California. He is also the author of *"The Cross & the Constitution in the Age of Incoherence,"* Tate Publishing, 2012.

While "tragedy" seems too small a word to describe the events at Newtown—or Aurora—let's not allow the liberal nannies rampant in our government and media to violate our Constitution in the pursuit of more security.

MORE GUN SILLINESS
FROM SENATOR FEINSTEIN

Written By Michell Zook

26 December 2012

Madame Feinstein—she of the brilliant "assault weapons" ban—has had another great idea this week. Why doesn't the United States, like Australia, buy back these prohibited weapons for something like $500 a gun, and then outlaw them?

There are more than a few problems with Senator Feinstein's thought. First and foremost, the Australians have nothing like our Bill of Rights, with its Second Amendment and the history behind it. But beyond the theoretical problems and the Supreme Court fight that would entail, a country that is on the verge of its own Greek-style fiscal crisis cannot possibly afford a buyback of this magnitude. Looking at the numbers, Australia's buyback program, consisting of semiautomatic guns, automatic guns and shotguns, cost their government $500 million in 1997. Using a 1% levy on income taxes, the government paid approximately $500 per gun.

How would this look in the United States? According to Gallup's most recent poll regarding gun ownership, 47% of 315 million Americans own guns, which means 148,050,000 Americans admit to owning guns. In Australia, one in four guns fell into the "banned" category, so using very simplified numbers, we'll assume each American admitting they own a gun only owns one. Continuing with our simplified numbers, we'll use the Aussie numbers of one in four being banned, so 37,012,500 would need to be bought back by the government. Even if the government only offers $500 per gun (which would be woefully under fair market value for many of these weapons), it would cost taxpayers $18,506,250,000. Keep in mind that the national debt is around $16 trillion. How are we supposed to pay for this, when the Senate can't even pass a budget?

Compare this $18.5 trillion cost to the cost of simply allowing teachers who already have valid concealed carry permits to carry in schools (with the two stipulations of the principal being aware of it and being required to keep the gun on your person at all times, as I mentioned last week), and a gun buyback program seems frivolous and more unnecessary government waste. Registration isn't the answer, not when we have newspapers publishing the names and addresses of gun owners—although it's certainly a burglar's dream, because then the people without guns suddenly have targets on their houses.

While "tragedy" seems too small a word to describe the events at Newtown—or Aurora—let's not allow the liberal nannies rampant in our government and media to violate our Constitution in the pursuit of more security. Even if the American government had the money to waste, any buyback would be a violation of the spirit of the Constitution. Our Founding Fathers intended for us to maintain weapons to protect against tyranny, not willingly surrender our weapons to obtain false security. So instead of coming up with knee-jerk solutions that would effectively treat a gunshot wound with a band-aid, why not solve the problem? We can blame the problem on guns, but what we're really seeing in America—and worldwide—is a breakdown in Judeo-Christian values and a willingness to accept individual responsibility.

No buyback can save people from themselves. No government can protect the people better than they can. It's time for the government to get back to its responsibilities outlined in the Constitution, just like it's time for parents to start being parents again, which means making sure their children are moral, healthy and fit for society. Until then, no gun law in America can protect us, which will be a great disappointment to Madame Feinstein.

About the Author

A native Texan currently living it up in Utah, Michelle served five years in the Air Force as an Air Battle Manager, attaining the rank of captain. These days, she's pursuing a MA Public Policy at Liberty University, learning the ropes as a military spouse, chasing two little ones around, staying caught up on the news, and trying not to meddle in her husband's career. She's a firm believer in states' rights, the Second Amendment and individual liberties.

"Dear God. We come before you with thanksgiving and praise. We thank you for another year without gun control and increased taxes. We thank you for healing Aunt Myrtle's gout and for miraculously removing Uncle Henry's goiter. Thanks for this food of which we are about to partake…"

It's a Hallowed, Gun-totin', Redneck Christmas

Written By Skip Coryell

27 December 2012

For years I've been telling people I'm a gun-totin' redneck. They always believe the gun-totin' part, but sometimes balk at the redneck label. I'm not exactly sure why; maybe because I don't fit the Jeff Foxworthy stereotype. After all, I can read and write, feed myself, and speak in more than one syllable without stuttering. Heck, I even have a college degree, and like I always say, "Ya give a redneck a college education 'n yer just askin' fer trouble."

So here I am, comfortable in my redneck roots, able to dine with kings and vagabonds with equal ease and grace. And that's never more apparent than during the holiday season when I go home to visit my kinfolk. I have five brothers and sisters and we always get together for the major holidays. Much of our celebrating is pretty average, and would fit in at any conservative, Christian home in America. But let's face it; some of it's not so normal.

Case in point: A few years back I was at my sister's house in the country. (All of us live in the country. We just don't fit in with city folk – way too many cops and restraining orders in the city.) I don't recall whether it was Thanksgiving or Christmas, just that it was deer season, which is a major holiday for all rednecks. The house was packed as usual. The men were talking guns, badmouthing liberals and taking their best guess on when society would collapse. The women were talking about the men, looking through the sale flyers in the local newspaper and comparing tattoos. The kids were busy testing out their muscles, trying to mix up gun powder and working out the pecking order. It was a pretty good day.

Once all the deviled eggs were eaten, we sat down at the table to feast on meat. We don't discriminate at the Coryell clan. Coryell's aren't like Jews or Arabs as we pretty much eat any kind of meat: cows, pigs, chickens, turkeys. (We don't even care if the animals are circumcised.) If it's not moving we cook it. If it is moving, then we shoot it. We have a very strict code of ethics: Never eat anything that's still alive; it just wouldn't be humane. It's like our own family version of PETA.

Being a God-fearing family, we all sat down around the table and bowed our heads to pray. It's always a solemn moment, because it's the only time Coryell's really shut their mouths. So all was quiet, and my brother-in-law began the turkey eulogy. "Dear God. We come before you with thanksgiving and praise. We thank you for another year without gun control and increased taxes. We thank you for healing Aunt Myrtle's gout and for miraculously removing Uncle Henry's goiter. Thanks for this food of which we are about to partake…"

But then I heard someone yell as loud as they could and everyone opened their eyes. "Hey! There's a buck out in that field!" In unison, as if working with the same brain, all the men jumped up and ran for a firearm. I was still loading my shotgun when I heard a window slide open and three shotgun blasts ring out. (Somehow gunshots always seem to sound louder inside a house.) I looked out the window and saw the six-pointer stumble, and then heard two more gunshots. The buck went down for the count and was soon taking the mother of all holiday dirt naps.

I unloaded my shotgun and put it back in the case as my brother-in-law went out to survey his prize. Several people complained that he shouldn't have left his shotgun loaded; it just wasn't fair. I'm an NRA instructor, so I was thinking It's just not safe. But, to be fair to my brother-in-law, it was his house and he was the fastest; and he was sitting closest to the window.

We all wandered back to the table and thanked God for the venison. Then we dug in and devoured anything that wasn't fast enough to get out of the way. It was a good holiday get together. Guns, God and family with an all-you-can-eat meat and potatoes buffet. Yes, God was good to us that year.

Okay, so if any of you out there still doubt my vaunted and coveted redneck status, well, when's the last time your family gunned down dinner from inside the house? Has your cousin ever shot off his left testicle? Does the ATF have your entire family tree on a permanent watch list? Have you ever body surfed behind a pick-up truck? I don't think so.

But let's not fight about it. After all; this is Christmas. Let's just all circle up, join hands and tell hunting stories. Merry Christmas. And yes, Jesus IS a life member of the NRA.

ABOUT THE AUTHOR

Skip Coryell lives with his wife and children in Michigan. Skip Coryell is the author of nine books including *Blood in the Streets: Concealed Carry and the OK Corral*, *RKBA: Defending the Right to Keep and Bear Arms*, *The God Virus*, and *We Hold These Truths*. He is the founder of The Second Amendment March, a Marine Corps veteran, and the President of White Feather Press. He is an avid hunter and sportsman, a Marine Corps veteran, and a graduate of Cornerstone University. For more details on Skip Coryell, or to contact him personally, go to his website at skipcoryell.com

To get a copy of Skip's latest novel *The Shadow Militia*, go to store.whitefeather-press.com or amazon.com.

Who gets to make the decision that firearms are no longer a legitimate hobby to collect, own, hunt with, target shoot, compete with and ultimately defend one's self and family with?

Senate Aiming for Our Guns

Written By Nathan Clark

28 December 2012

Perennial hypocrite Senator Dianne Feinstein from the Insane Peoples' Republic of California is coming after guns – again. She has a history of attacking the Second Amendment's foundations with attempts to demonize certain types of firearms and seeking legislation banning sales and possession of guns. She is also registered to carry a concealed firearm. It's okay for her, but you're not trustworthy.

A well-intended citizen might read her newest proposal, penned in the aftermath of the Newtown tragedy, and think that the provisions therein don't seem that extreme. We all want to be safe, right? Nobody wants to live in the "wild West" that Democrats love to invoke when discussing "gun reform". I mean, who really needs an "assault rifle" besides the military? Why should ordinary citizens have access to military-style weaponry and all the accoutrements? Never mind that those weapons don't have the same capability as the ones issued to our soldiers. They "look" scary, so ban them. The same goes for magazine sizes. Who needs seventeen or thirty-shot capacity?

These seemingly reasonable questions raise one that is infinitely more concerning; who decides what is enough and which firearms "'look" harmless enough to "allow" the public to own them? Who gets to make the decision that firearms are no longer a legitimate hobby to collect, own, hunt with, target shoot, compete with and ultimately defend one's self and family with?

The reason this is a critically important question is because that person or persons who make those decisions will accrue an enormous amount of power unto themselves, perhaps the kind that cannot be restrained. They also will be empowered with changing or eradicating part of the Bill of Rights, which does not derive its power from the government but rather stands as the last bulwark against excessive government power. It is of crucial importance not to succumb to knee-jerk legislation every time some tragedy happens. Good law never results from high emotions.

Let's take one of the most seemingly innocuous parts of Feinstein's proposed bill and examine its potential consequences. Her proposal calls for a retroactive national registry of all existing gun owners, so the government will know who every gun owner is and what they have in their possession at all times. Perhaps the "intent" of this action is to ensure that firearms don't wind up in the wrong hands, such as felons, the mentally unstable or even Mexican drug lords. Here's where it becomes a two-fold problem.

The first issue is how much the government has a right to know about private citizens. Historically, gun registration has led to gun confiscation, followed closely by either a spike in crime rates or a despotic government abusing and killing its own citizens. People who pooh-pooh this are willfully ignorant of world history. The facts are there, and the body counts are terrifyingly high.

The second issue with registration is that collected and stored information, especially sensitive information about private citizens, can be accessed and broadcast to the world (and unsavory recipients) in a matter of seconds. Wikileaks exists because of this fact. Once the information is out there, there's no calling it back.

A glaring example of this abuse of private information happened this week. *The Journal News*, a Gannett publication based in White Plains, NY published a list of 44,000 legal gun owners in two New York counties, complete with their names and addresses. They even went so far as to use Google Maps to show exactly where those owners live. The newspaper obtained this government data through the Freedom of Information Act, and plans to publish another New York county's roster next week as well. The private citizens on the list were all compliant with New York's strict gun registry law, and here is the net result. If such a registry did not exist, this highly-private and potentially damaging information would not be available for such abuse.

Legal gun owners are just as dismayed at the events in Colorado, Arizona, Virginia Tech and Newtown as anybody else. We do not want firearms in the wrong hands, especially those of criminals and deranged individuals. Neither do we believe that running gunfights in the streets are any way to establish or maintain the peace. However, wholesale gutting of the Second Amendment serves no one's purposes except twisted politicians and criminals, and they are intentionally mentioned in the same sentence. There are federal, state and local laws in place to prevent guns getting to criminals, and somebody needs to step up and get involved with mental illness intervention and prevent access to firearms for those who are unstable of mind.

In each of the aforementioned shootings, the perpetrator was clearly known to be deranged by those close to them, and nothing was said or done to prevent what followed. Their isolation was abetted by the inaction and inattention of those closest. That's not an opinion, it is a fact.

With Feinstein's national gun registry, millions of proven law-abiding gun owners are but an FOIA request away from being "outed" to the criminal public. Not to mention one act of government away from confiscation and persecution. Nobody would be safer as a result. Not even Senator Feinstein.

ABOUT THE AUTHOR

Nathan Clark is a conservative commentator who resides with his wife in New Hampshire. He is passionate about preserving the vision of our nation's Founders and advancing those tried and true principles deep into America's future. His interests range broadly from flyfishing, cooking and shooting to pro sports, gardening, live music and fine-scale modeling.

Then it happened, my first hint that things in our world had changed. I lay my two carbines on the conveyor belt with pride. I noticed the couple behind me looking at my purchase. The woman kind of shook her head, and the man quickly glanced away. I thought that was odd, but I didn't care. Then the lady behind the register scanned the first rifle. I was still giddy. She grabbed the second one and actually shuddered a bit and said, "These look vicious!"

Gun Control ... Even BB Guns? – Really?

By S.C. Sherman

29 December 2012

One of the most famous and iconic pieces of American movie masterpieces is the 1983 comedy *A Christmas Story*. Especially known for one of the most memorable quotes ever, when the main character asks Santa for a Red Ryder Carbine for Christmas. Santa responds, "You'll shoot your eye out kid!" The movie taps into one of the fondest memories of many a young American – to actually be trusted with the awesome power of a BB gun as a Christmas gift. And not just any BB gun, a Red Ryder lever action carbine. Oh yeah, what's better than that?

I recently found myself strolling the aisles of the evil retailer known as Wal-Mart. I stopped and stared at an entire end cap full of The Original Red Ryder BB guns. Images of my youth flashed through my head and my pulse quickened. I knew this was the perfect gift for my boys, ages 11 and 7. I noticed they'd even added a version with a pink stock for the girls! Anyway, my youngest daughter is too young.

I reached for one the legendary firearms as a vision of my two boys fighting over it filled my thoughts. I could just see them, one holding the butt, one the barrel, tugging and yelling as lessons of sharing vanished into thin air. I grabbed another carbine. Yep, one for each boy, might as well arm them both, right? I was so excited for them I smiled all the way to the front where I encountered a serpentine line that extended a quarter mile to one of the forty cashiers! Oh well, even Christmas lines couldn't wipe that smile off my face. With this gift I envisioned my boys growing into manhood. I was inviting my little fellas up into the world of weapons. A real weapon, not a toy.

Then it happened, my first hint that things in our world had changed. I lay my two carbines on the conveyor belt with pride. I noticed the couple behind me looking at my purchase. The woman kind of shook her head, and the man quickly glanced away. I thought that was odd, but I didn't care. Then the lady behind the register scanned the first rifle. I was still giddy. She grabbed the second one and actually shuddered a bit and said, "These look vicious!" At first I thought she was kidding, but then I realized she wasn't. I quickly put my Assault BB guns in my cart and mumbled something like, "They're just BB guns…"

I suddenly became uneasy and glanced over my shoulder. I wondered if I was being watched or if I'd just been placed on some kind of list. I cursed myself for using a credit card. I could see the outer doors as I held my breath wondering if I'd make it out before I was ushered back into some other room to be interrogated. I made it to my car and sped away checking my mirrors regularly. About half way home, I calmed down, realizing I was overreacting. BB guns are like Apple Pie and Baseball. Right?

Just to make myself feel better I quickly posted on a social networking site about my new purchase. I expected many people to chime in and tell me what a great gift it would be for my sons. Well, I got a couple of responses like that; followed with a nice argument about the gun violence I was promoting and the benefits of Australian gun control. I must admit I was starting to get a bit edgy and was almost looking for a fight. I began to wonder, *What's happened to the America of my youth?* Have we really gone so far in just my few years that a mere BB gun invites deridation? I shook it off. It couldn't be true.

Christmas came and both my boys literally jumped with joy and hugged their old dad with true love as they opened their new carbines. I felt a kindred bond as they couldn't wait to get to my parent's farm the next day to shoot their new weapons. My older boy got distracted with his cousin and the pool table, as my younger son begged me to go out shooting. I was so proud. We discussed the safety features of his new weapon, loaded it with eco-friendly copper BB's, promised his mother not to damage anything or shoot out any eyes, and we set out as men. It was awesome.

We shot a few targets at pretty close range. A few bulls eye's can really build your confidence no matter what your age.

"Hey, you want to try to shoot a bird or something?" I asked. His eyes sparkled with the hope of his first hunt. We stalked the farm yard and found a bunch of sparrows behind the barn. He took careful aim and fired. The sound was deafening and the rifle leapt in his arms, okay maybe not, but anyway.

"I got him!" my son hollered. I was stunned.

"Really?" I said trying not to sound shocked. Sure enough, he had bagged himself a sparrow on his first try. Talk about pride. We ran to the house to show everyone his first kill. My son and I walked back outside.

"Well, you're a real hunter now," I said.

"Really?" he replied. "Thanks Dad. I love you." We hugged and it was about as good as it gets for just an instant. Later on that day, I decided to go ahead and post my photo of the mighty hunter and his quarry, with his newly tested weapon.

It was a great photo; you'd have thought it was the trophy of a lifetime as my little man beamed ear to ear. I knew the risk I was taking by posting it, but I'm tired of hiding who we are, so I hit post. All went well for awhile.

Then I got an email from a friend suggesting I take down my picture because it could cause me to get in trouble from the Department of Natural Resources. Worried, that we'd broken some law. We hadn't, sparrows are still free game, for now. I can't even count how many sparrows I killed as a boy, and here I was worried that we might get in trouble over one. Wondering if we even had the right to shoot one of the King's birds?

Not a single new law has passed, but the societal changes have begun. Every day I hear of new ideas on how to restrict all of us who didn't do a thing to hurt anyone. Assault weapons bans, mandatory buy-back programs, outright confiscation of certain arms, ammo, magazines, muzzle breaks, collapsible stocks, and on and on. None of those ideas will make us one bit safer from crazy people intent on death. My experience with the harmless BB gun showed me that the attack upon our freedom to bear arms is much more pervasive than the headlines lead us to believe. The attempt to change the fabric of our society is slower and more insidious, but effective nonetheless. If you think I'm wrong, let your kid ride a bike around without a helmet. You'll see how powerful shifts in society can be.

Things are definitely different than they were when I was a boy. I for one don't think different is always better. One thing remains the same. Little boys still like to shoot BB guns! Nothing will ever change that. Not all of the battle is fought with laws. Push back hard – buy a kid a BB gun!

ABOUT THE AUTHOR

S.C. Sherman grew up a farm kid in rural Iowa. He graduated from the University of Iowa with a degree in Communications Studies. Steve is a business owner, and recently ran for Iowa State House of Representatives.. S.C. enjoys political commentary and great stories. He has written three fiction novels found at www.scsherman.com He currently lives with his wife and four children in North Liberty, Iowa.

Ah, who am I kidding? The Assault Weapons Ban didn't work. School shootings shot through the roof, and lo and behold killers still found a way around the uber-strict regulations to carry out their death wishes with an assortment of weapons. Yep, correct me if I'm wrong, but I believe the biggest spike in school shootings in our nation's short history occurred during the initial AWB.

The Assault Weapons Ban Didn't Work Then and It Won't Work Now

Written By Doug Giles

30 December 2012

Senator Dianne Feinstein is queuing up come January 2013 to retable-yet again-an Assault Weapons Ban (AWB) in order to "severely mitigate the possibilities of another Sandy Hook atrocity." Great idea, Dianne, as the first AWB that Clinton signed into law worked wonders in schools from 1994-2004. It was awesome. It panned out wonderfully aside from the following:

- November 7, 1994: Wickliffe, Ohio: (Wickliffe Middle School shooting) ~~Name deleted~~, 37, a former student at the school, shot and killed custodian Pete Christopher and wounded four other adults.

- January 12, 1995: Seattle, Washington: A 15-year-old Garfield High School student left school during the day and returned with his grandfather's 9mm semiautomatic handgun. He wounded two students.

- October 12, 1995: Blackville, South Carolina: (Blackville-Hilda High School shooting) ~~Name deleted~~, 16, killed one teacher and wounded another before committing suicide.

- November 15, 1995: Lynnville, Tennessee: (Richland High School shooting) ~~Name deleted~~, 17, killed a student and teacher and seriously wounded another teacher with a .22-caliber rifle.

- February 2, 1996: Moses Lake, Washington: (Frontier Middle School shooting) ~~Name deleted~~, 14, killed a teacher and two students and wounded another student when he opened fire on his algebra class.

- August 15, 1996: San Diego, California: (San Diego State University shooting) Name deleted, a 36-year-old graduate student killed three professors that he believed were involved in a conspiracy against him.

- September 17, 1996: State College, Pennsylvania: (Hetzel Union Building shooting) Name deleted, 19, shoots and kills one student and injures two outside.

- February 19, 1997: Bethel, Alaska: Bethel Regional High School student Name deleted, 16, shot and killed the school's principal and one student, and wounded two other students.

- October 1, 1997: Pearl, Mississippi: (Pearl High School shooting) Name deleted, 16, murdered his mother at home before killing his ex-girlfriend and another student and wounding seven others at Pearl High School. He and his friends were said to be outcasts who worshiped Satan.

- November 27, 1997: West Palm Beach, Florida: Conniston Middle School student Name deleted, 14, fatally shot Johnpierre Kamel, 14, outside school after an argument over a wristwatch.

- December 1, 1997: West Paducah, Kentucky: (Heath High School shooting) Three students were killed and five wounded by Name deleted, 14, as they participated in a prayer circle.

- December 15, 1997: Stamps, Arkansas: Name deleted, 14, concealed in a wooded area on school grounds, shoots and wounds two students as they were entering Stamps High School.

- March 24, 1998: Craighead County, Arkansas: Name deleted, 13, and Name deleted, 11, killed four students and one teacher and wounded ten others as Westside Middle School emptied during a fire alarm intentionally set off by Golden.

- April 24, 1998: Edinboro, Pennsylvania (Parker Middle School dance shooting) Name deleted, 14, fatally shot teacher John Gillette, 48, and wounded two students and a teacher at an 8th grade graduation dance.

- May 19, 1998: Fayetteville, Tennessee: Name deleted, 18, shoots Robert Creson, 18, in a dispute over a girl.

- May 21, 1998: Springfield, Oregon: After killing his parents at home, Name deleted, 15, drove to Thurston High School where he shot and killed two students and wounded 25 others.

- June 15, 1998: Richmond, Virginia: A 14-year-old student of Armstrong High School wounds a teacher and a school volunteer.

- December 10, 1998: Detroit, Michigan: Professor Andrzej Olbrot is killed by graduate student Name deleted, 48.

- April 20, 1999: Littleton, Colorado: (Columbine High School massacre) Name deleted, 18, and Name deleted, 17, killed 12 students and one teacher, and wounded 21 others before committing suicide at Columbine High School.

- May 20, 1999: Conyers, Georgia: (Heritage High School shooting) Six students injured by Name deleted., 15.

- November 19, 1999: Deming, New Mexico: A 13-year-old girl fatally shot at Deming Middle School by Name deleted., 13. He stated he had intended to commit suicide but was jostled by others and the gun moved.

- February 29, 2000: Elementary School, Flint, Michigan: 6-year-old Name deleted, youngest-ever school shooter. Kayla Rolland was the single fatality.

- May 26, 2000: Lake Worth, Florida: Lake Worth Middle School Florida teacher Barry Grunow was fatally shot by his student, 13-year-old Name deleted, who had returned to school after being sent home at 1 p.m. by the assistant principal for throwing water balloons. He returned to school on his bike with a 5-inch Raven and four bullets stolen from his grandfather the week before. He was an honor student. Grunow was a popular teacher and the murderer's favorite.

- August 28, 2000: University of Arkansas shooting at Fayetteville, Arkansas: At approximately 12:14 pm, Dr. John R. Locke, 67, Director of the Comparative Literature Program was shot and killed in his office by Name deleted, 36, a Comparative Literature PhD candidate who had recently been dismissed from the program for lack of progress toward his degree. Name deleted shot Dr. Locke three times before taking his own life in Dr. Locke's office after it was cordoned off by campus police.

- September 26, 2000: Name deleted, 13, offender in Louisiana school shooting with 1 student fatality.

- March 5, 2001: Name deleted, age 15, offender in California school shooting at Santana High School, 15 wounded 2 of whom died.

- March 30, 2001: Name deleted., age 18, offender in Indiana school shooting with 1 student fatality.

- September 24, 2003: Name deleted, age 15, offender in Minnesota school shooting with 2 student fatalities.

- February 2, 2004: Unidentified offender in Washington, DC school shooting with 1 student fatality.

- May 7, 2004: Unidentified 17-year-old offender in Maryland school shooting with 1 student fatality.

And that's excluding the Fairchild Air Force Base Massacre in 1994; the Alfred P. Murrah Federal Building Massacre in 1995; the Caltrans Maintenance Yard Massacre in 1997; the Connecticut State Lottery Headquarters Massacre in 1998; the Wedgewood Baptist Church Massacre of 1999; the Xerox Office Building Massacre in 1999; the Edgewater Technology Office Massacre in 2000; and the September 11, 2001 terrorist attacks which killed nearly 3,000 people (in which the culprits used box cutters and airplanes to pull that one off). We should have had an Assault Box Cutter and Airplane Ban in place I guess.

Yep, excluding the aforementioned, the AWB that the Left put into practice nearly two decades ago really mitigated murderous schoolyard and workplace evil for its ten-year run, right?

Ah, who am I kidding? The Assault Weapons Ban didn't work. School shootings shot through the roof, and lo and behold killers still found a way around the uber-strict regulations to carry out their death wishes with an assortment of weapons. Yep, correct me if I'm wrong, but I believe the biggest spike in school shootings in our nation's short history occurred during the initial AWB. Google it and get back to me.

Oh, and another thing according to a comprehensive Congressional Research Service report on guns and gun control legislation: Less than 2% of 203,300 state and federal prisoners who were armed during the crime for which they were incarcerated "used, carried, or possessed a semiautomatic assault weapon." If the hooligans did use a gun it was mostly your normal, non-funky firearm, i.e. mostly hunting guns and non-"assault" weapons. But we can rest assured that the Progressives would never come after our Remington 870s and our revolvers (because they promised). Never. Ever. Ever.

In addition to the AWB not really stemming the tide of gun violence in the public school systems, it sure didn't calm things down in the "gun-free" Windy City, as Chi-town racked up a whopping 7,636 murders during the Clinton ban.

Speaking of Chicago, this year alone 446 kids have been shot where guns have been verboten, and just this week Chicago hit 500 murders that have now occurred in the "gun free" Toddlin' Town for 2012.

It appears as if our former AWB and our current "gun free" zones don't work.

About Doug Giles

Doug Giles is the man behind ClashDaily.com. In addition to driving ClashDaily.com, Giles is a popular columnist on Townhall.com and the author of the book Raising Righteous & Rowdy Girls.

Doug's articles have also appeared on several other print and online news sources, including The Washington Times, The Daily Caller, Fox Nation, USA Today, The Wall Street Journal, The Washington Examiner, The Blaze, American Hunter Magazine and ABC News.

He's been a frequent guest on the Fox News Channel and Fox Business Channel as well as many nationally syndicated radio shows across the nation — which, he believes, officially makes him a super hero.

In addition, Doug is an occasional guest host on New York City's WABC (The Jason Mattera Show) and he is a weekly guest, every Friday at 7:45am[et], on America's Morning News (155 markets).

Giles and his wife Margaret have two daughters: Hannah, who devastated ACORN with her 2009 nation shaking undercover videos, and Regis who is an NRA columnist, huntress and Second Amendment activist.

DG's interests include guns, big game hunting, big game fishing, fine art, cigars, helping wounded warriors, and being a big pain in the butt to people who dislike God and the USA.

Read more Doug Giles at www.clashdaily.com.

Soon enough, if this gun-control legislation passes, those very guns the young girls used to protect their lives will be illegal and the little bambinas who defended their lives would go to jail for shooting a person in self-defense with an "illegal" gun.

Little Bambinas and Jackass Shooters

Written By Regis Giles

30 December 2012

Earlier this year there were news headlines breaking that little girls defended their lives and homestead from douche bag intruders by taking their parent's firearm and blasting the guy out the door.

If you remember my CPAC speech, you will know that I am very happy about this.

These girls, because their parents taught them at a young age how to shoot, defended their innocence, protected their lives and are still alive today instead of belly up in some back-woods creek.

With stories like these, you would think our legislators would be happy and rejoice over the fact that those girls had a gun to protect their lives. You would think they would wake up and realize guns in the hands of good people are helpful to human societies.

However, with recent events that have taken place, the Sandy Hook massacre, politicians aren't letting this tragedy pass without pushing their gun-control agenda.

Yes, some may argue their agenda only addresses gun magazines that hold a certain number of ammunition or semi-automatic rifles. Supporters would say, "They aren't really asking for much, just those few minor changes, which will have an immense effect on gun violence." However, every inch of gun rights the gun-control zealots take away from "we the people" is a step towards slavery.

Soon enough, if this gun-control legislation passes, those very guns the young girls used to protect their lives will be illegal and the little bambinas who defended their lives would go to jail for shooting a person in self-defense with an "illegal" gun.

The fact that more restrictive laws have to be added, after some psycho maniac allegedly broke 40 some laws in executing his plan of destruction, is a ridiculous notion.

Sandy Hook Massacre

This is not the "Land of the Free" that I remember, this is not the "Land of the Free" our Founders intended, and the America that the gun-control advocates are proposing is not the "Land of the Free" I read about in the history books.

About the Author

Regis Giles is the creator and owner of Girls Just Wanna Have Guns.com and is a leading voice for Second Amendment rights, self-defense and conservationism. Unafraid to speak her mind, Regis takes no prisoners. Her media appearances include: ELLE Magazine, The Daily Mail, ABC, CNN, & Fox News.

America's gun culture, I praise it; I enjoy it. I honor it. I celebrate it. I am proud of it. I write stories about it. I often spend my leisure hours participating in it. I fill my freezer and my belly with it.

Not Ashamed of America's Gun Culture

Written By R.G. Yoho

31 December 2012

The other day in our local newspaper, there were three political columns on the editorial page, all three of them one-sidedly calling for gun control and moaning about America's "Gun Culture."

As a law-abiding gun owner, I must say that I am a part of America's gun culture. I am proud of it. In addition, I often thank God for it.

During World War II, the most brutal fighting experienced by our military were the battles waged against the Japanese Imperial Army. Moreover, the inhumane conditions faced by our captured American POWs and the atrocities visited upon them by their Japanese captors was like nothing faced by most of those in German prison camps.

On Iwo Jima, over 7,000 American soldiers were killed, some of them forced to engage in hand-to-hand combat. About that same number of Americans lost their life at Guadalcanal.

Therefore, one can only wonder how many Americans — civilians and military alike — would have died had the Japanese chosen to invade the mainland of the United States.

Japanese General Yamamoto said, "You cannot invade the mainland United States. There would be a rifle behind every blade of grass."

Their decision not to invade the United States was a direct result of what they believed to be America's "gun culture."

Therefore, you should thank God for it too.

During that same time, the Japanese invaded China, a nation without a gun culture.

In Nanking, the Japanese killed over 250,000 civilians.

Soldiers deliberately raped women in front of their husbands. They forced fathers to rape their own daughters. They forced sons to rape their mothers. Moreover, they killed any family member who tried to intervene.

The Japanese soldiers impaled infants on their bayonets, tossing them back and forth, spearing their bleeding, lifeless, tiny bodies on their guns like it was a game.

And had Yamamoto chosen to invade our mainland, then you would have seen the same nearly-unspeakable atrocities occurring right in the streets of America.

You should thank God for our gun culture.

Nearly every nation that practiced gun control has eventually seen their citizens wiped out in acts of mass murder or genocide.

The same thing would happen here as well.

As a Western author, some would say I write stories that glorify America's gun culture. As a gun owner and hunter, I proudly exercise my right to engage in America's gun culture. As an American who respects the Constitution our Founders penned for us, I also celebrate our gun culture.

America's gun culture, I praise it; I enjoy it. I honor it. I celebrate it. I am proud of it. I write stories about it. I often spend my leisure hours participating in it. I fill my freezer and my belly with it.

America's gun culture, I believe God instituted it, our Founders gave everything to establish it, and our military often died to protect it.

I believe in America's gun culture.

So should you!

About the Author

Author R.G. Yoho is the author of three Westerns, including "Death Comes to Redhawk."

In addition to his Westerns, R.G. recently published a work of non-fiction, "America's History is His Story."

Please check out his Author's Page on Facebook: http://www.Facebook.com/R.G.Yoho

*Liberals want power. All of it. If we continue to ignore
this fact we are handing it to them. If we allow the Second
Amendment to be circumvented, driven out of existence, we
won't need to ask "How will it all end?" It's already over.*

Gun Control and Sandy Crooks

Written By Marilyn Assenheim

3 January 2013

Oh, how will it all end? Duh.

The close of 2012 and beginning of the New Year contained enough appalling activity, aided and abetted by elected Republicans, to have warranted the suicide of old 2012 and kept 2013's New Year baby desperately scrabbling to stay in the womb. The list is far too lengthy to itemize everything but here are some of the highlights:

- Our Secretary of State's case of Benghazi Flu and subsequent hospitalization for a "blood clot" situated in some undisclosed location of her carcass.

- The anointing of John Kerry as her probable successor (another "thank you" will be due to Senator McCain very soon).

- Congress voting to postpone the "fiscal cliff 'by raising taxes across the board … about 77% of households are affected (surprise, surprise). The bill does not limit spending, provides billions of dollars in tax credits for the likes of Hollywood producers, Puerto Rico, rum companies, NASCAR and algae growers and ups the national debt by another $4 trillion ("Yea" votes for this pig's breakfast included that of our intrepid fiscal hero and recent Vice Presidential nominee, Paul Ryan). Congress never read the bill. The Senate got the bill 3 minutes before voting on it. Next fiscal cliff? February 2013.

- No demand for a budget. "Nuff said.

- A $60 billion dollar bill for hurricane Sandy … which includes beneficiaries like Alaskan fisheries. The Vacationer in Chief neglected to sign it because he was scrambling to get back to Hawaii this week … at a taxpayer cost of an additional $7 million, and will probably sign it via autopen.

- An all-out attack on the Second Amendment. It is this item that may be the final nail in our coffin.

- The Sandy Hook calamity led to a surprising response from Americans, nationwide. A recent Gallup poll stated that 74% of Americans want gun ownership to be left alone. According to the FBI, requests for background checks for gun ownership hit a new, record high in December, 2012 (2.8 million), up from the previous high in November, 2012 (2 million). Statistics continue to accumulate, are published, yet continue to be ignored by the media and the ruling class, proving that gun ownership by law-abiding individuals inhibits crime.

Hollywood celebutards are being ridiculed for their hypocritical PC stance on gun control when their on-screen presence glorifies irresponsible gun use. Interviews with Sandy Hook residents clearly put the problem where it should be: Not on gun ownership but on controlling the insane. Recent problems in New York City should make this patently clear. Two people, at last count, have been shoved under moving subway cars during the past week. What should be done about it? Prohibit subway transportation? Yet, Mayor-For-Life Bloomberg claims there's nothing to see here.

California just experienced a "boom" in gun ownership and the result was that the crime rates dropped. Yet, despite America's clearly expressed desire to have gun ownership left alone what do we get? Piers "he's-your-problem-now" Morgan, CNN's noted Constitutional expert by way of England, illegally deriding our Constitution and Napoleonic sports clown, Bob Costas, going off on a characteristically, ill-informed, anti-gun rant during a football game. Gun owners are "outed" in the press, hyper, liberal bleating and a Congress determined to squeeze more citizens' rights out of existence. And this one is the Rosetta Stone of rights.

Senator Diane Feinstein wants yet another bill passed against gun ownership. She has, chillingly, stated that she wants all private gun ownership outlawed. The president said he is going after guns in 2013. And the Lyin' King hasn't even been sworn in yet.

If we continue to insist that liberal demands for gun control are merely a "difference of opinion" or are born of "good intentions" we will continue to miss the point. Liberals want power. All of it. If we continue to ignore this fact we are handing it to them. If we allow the Second Amendment to be circumvented, driven out of existence, we won't need to ask "How will it all end?" It's already over.

ABOUT THE AUTHOR

Marilyn Assenheim was born and raised in New York City. She is a first generation American. Her parents were Holocaust survivors and LEGAL immigrants to this great country. She spent a career in healthcare management although she probably should have been a casting director or a cowboy. She is a serious devotee of history and politics, Marilyn currently lives in the NYC metropolitan area.

"The President, Vice President and all civil Officers of the United States, shall be removed from Office on Impeachment for, and Conviction of, Treason, Bribery, or other high Crimes and Misdemeanors." ~ Article II, Section 4 of the United States Constitution

Obama's Gun Control Presidential Threat is Impeachable Offense

Written By Kevin Fobbs

3 January 2013

This weekend the President of the United States declared war on legitimate gun owners who have the protection of the U.S. Constitution under their Second Amendment rights. Barack Obama informed the host of *Meet the Press* on the December 27th show and its viewing audience that he would use the full authority and "full weight" of the presidential arsenal of his office to unleash the dogs of war against legal gun owners.

The threat is real, because if one considers the nature of Obama's cavalier attitude toward upholding or even recognizing the legitimacy of the authority of the U.S. Constitution, he has little regard for it. He has ignored the 10th Amendment regarding state's rights, the Second Amendment regarding gun rights, and even laws passed by congress, like the Defense of Marriage Act. His presidency has been a renegade take-over and emasculation of the very constitution he swore to uphold.

The course of action is clear for the Congress of the United States: the President of the United States has decided to pursue a direction that even the U.S. Supreme Court in 2008 and 2010 cases, has concluded is legally without merit. The president believes through his actions that the Second Amendment can be marginalized, and with the full consent of a weakened congress, that gives in to his pressure as it did on January 1st with the Fiscal Cliff bill.

What is left to wonder for Americans to weigh about the need for impeachment proceedings as guaranteed under the U.S. Constitution. There is nothing left to debate, to discuss, to bargain or barter over. An assault on freedom and the constitution regarding gun rights is not open for negotiation or for misinterpretation.

Impeachment hearings are a serious step for any congress to consider, and it takes a matter which is defined by the U.S. Constitution as impeachable offenses for judiciary hearings to be undertaken by the House of Representatives.

Three sitting presidents have been investigated by congress, which had impeachment charges brought against them, beginning with President Andrew Johnson in 1867, Richard Nixon in 1974, and Bill Clinton in 1998. In each of the cases, the three presidents attempted to thwart either the will of the legislative branch, lied to the legislative branch or mislead the legislative branch in open and contemptible violation of the law.

Yet, in each case there was not an attempt to openly circumvent the constitutional authority of congress or eliminate constitutional protections guaranteed by the U.S. Constitution, as Obama has engaged in. This sitting president has engaged in such actions as defined by the Constitution's framers as well as those states that approved this essential American document.

The impeachment investigation by congress is a critical and necessary first step:

"Those who adopted the Constitution viewed impeachment as a remedy for usurpation or abuse of power or serious breach of trust. …Thus, the impeachment power of the House reaches "those who behave amiss, or betray their public trust," according to the Washington Post's "Constitutional Grounds for Presidential Impeachment".

The betrayal of the public trust is a key component that elevates Obama's conduct, both past and present, to this impeachment threshold. By engaging in continuing dismissive conduct regarding selective enforcement of the laws of the United States he bears congressional investigation. He has therefore "betrayed the public trust", by these actions that the framers of the U.S. Constitution felt warranted impeachment of the nation's highest constitutional officer.

"The President, Vice President and all civil Officers of the United States, shall be removed from Office on Impeachment for, and Conviction of, Treason, Bribery, or other high Crimes and Misdemeanors." – Article II, Section 4 of the United States Constitution

Let the first action of the new congress be one which serves notice on the re-elected president, that due to high crimes and misdemeanors you are so charged with Impeachment!

About the Author

Kevin Fobbs has more than 35 years of wide-ranging experience as a community and tenant organizer, Legal Services outreach program director, public relations consultant, business executive, gubernatorial and presidential appointee, political advisor, widely published writer, and national lecturer. Kevin is co-chair and co-founder of AC-3 (American-Canadian Conservative Coalition) that focuses on issues on both sides of the border between the two countries.

...while we do owe the King certain things, if that King comes through the front door to rape my wife, he is no longer a king – he's a rapist and the right thing to do is to draw your sword and to run him through.

Top Two Reasons to Own a Gun: Thank God and Sam Colt

Written By John Kirkwood

4 January 2013

My right to own a gun, to stroke it, to use it, and to pass it on to my children is not a matter of pragmatism, so I'm not going to argue statistics or polls, even though they'd be in my favor. And this list is in no particular order because, after the top two reasons, it really doesn't matter how you order the rest. It's like the top musical acts of the twentieth century; there's Elvis and the Beatles and where you rank The Stones, The Who or Led Zeppelin is just a matter of preference. In this case, the top two reasons to own a gun are to "shoot a bastard" and to "shoot a tyrant," or at least to have the capacity.

Yes, I like poking holes in paper at 1100 feet per second and I love to take a pheasant down with my Remington 870, but "sport" and "hunting" are not the reasons that our Founders were so "fanatical" about gun rights. Guns are also a great investment and in the Obama age, that's a rare commodity, so it cracks the top ten. Want a good return on your investment, buy gold; want a good return on your freedom – buy lead. Still, not in the top two. I even like to stare at the guns in my collection and to see the "O" face of my friends when they eye-fondle my antique Winchester rifle; but our fathers didn't risk lives, fortunes, and sacred honor for my right to display museum pieces. So let's get to the meat of the matter, shall we?

Guns are meant to kill. Amen! They're a tool made for killing. As a tool they can be used rightly or wrongly, and in the commission of justice or malice, but most of the time, they're never used at all. Killing animals is good for the belly and can give you an appreciation for God's creation, the food chain and the Noahic Covenant; hunting can even increase the bond between individuals, but it's not imprimis.

Killing bad guys is; it is good for the soul, the neighborhood, the nation and the universe. Killing bad guys is even good for the ungrateful, pacifist, worm that kvetches at the sight of four tweens playing Risk (because of the implied "conflict"). He doesn't know it because he's never read Orwell beyond the stripped and bleached quotes from The Daily Kos, but it is true, "people sleep peaceably in their beds at night only because rough men stand ready to do violence on their behalf."

One reason to own a gun is because you can. We're Americans. The right to KEEP and BEAR guns is our heritage. Dianne Feinstein and Mayor Bloomberg may want us to barter that right away for a bowl of lentils, but our "right" transcends the 2nd Amendment. The Founders didn't grant the right to us; they simply recognized that as free men, we have that right. God gave us the right to protect and defend our lives and our property. We have not ceded that right to the policeman, the soldier or the politician; we have extended that right to them.

To Kill a Bastard:

Personal defense is high on the list and because I live outside of Chicago, I know a thing or two about out-of-control violent crime in the face of draconian, stringent gun laws. Oh, I don't mean an illegitimate child, here. By "bastard," I mean a guy who tries to eat you on a Miami highway or tries to kick in the basement window to get jiggy with your five year old. The meth-head that would tie you up and light you on fire, just to get $25 for his next OMG, is a bastard; so is anyone who would separate you from your money, your children, or your heartbeat.

Another great reason to own a gun is because I'm not Chuck Norris or Barack Obama – ghosts don't sit around the campfire telling "John Kirkwood" stories and I don't have a personal Secret Service detail, so I'll have to settle for my H&K .45. Colt gave us the great equalizer, a tool that could put Pee-Wee Herman on equal ground with Conan the Barbarian and civilization is better for it.

There's something to say about those countries that have disarmed only to be faced with hundreds of thousands of bastards arriving on troop carriers. During World War II, the defenseless British begged the U.S. for arms and thousands of Americans sent their family shotguns and hunting rifles to aid the Limeys in their defense against Nazi bastards.

Personal defense and national defense are damn good reasons to be armed, to be armed well and to be as proficient as the average Hollywood hypocrite who makes a living playing with a gun, is protected by guys with guns and then makes PSAs about taking our guns away.

To Kill a Tyrant:

"America is at that awkward stage. It's too late to work within the system, but too early to shoot the bastards." ~ Claire Wolfe

This is the top dog! Thank God for lead and gun powder or we'd still be living as serfs under a feudal lord. Our Founders developed a healthy respect for an armed populace and gleaned their wisdom from guys like Samuel Rutherford. Rutherford wrote LEX REX (Law is King), and it was the garlic necklace to the vampire doctrine of the divine right of kings. He suggests that, while we do owe the King certain things, if that King comes through the front door to rape my wife, he is no longer a king – he's a rapist and the right thing to do is to draw your sword and to run him through.

My Bushmaster is my sword. If our "representatives" make good on their threats to confiscate guns, then it'll be time to draw the sword. I respect ballots and so did the Founders, but we don't live in freedom today because Sam Adams and Patrick Henry cast a ballot. Our Founders stuffed a musket because the English were stuffing the ballots and as a free man, I retain my right to water the Tree of Liberty if tyranny should arise on my watch.

If that time comes in our generation, then we'll find out what we're made of. Christians are fond of quoting Paul's aphorism, "for me to live is Christ" but when choosing between living by that statement and dying or even discomfort, the herd thins. "From my cold dead hands" is a witticism, a quip, but one day it may be a necessity. Pasting the bumper sticker on your Facebook wall or your Ford F-150 is one thing; living and dying by it is quite another. The pen may be mightier than the sword, but an armed populace is mightier than a tyrant's pen.

My AR-15 is freedom's spade. It is the main tool in Liberty's toolbox; the ultimate "just in case" if my generation would need to lay a new foundation. There are those in this country and many in this administration that would like to strip us of our guns, not to protect children, but to accumulate power. It is why they won't listen to reason; it is why, in the face of contrary evidence, they turn their head and it is why they have a speech and a bill ready to be spewed out on command whenever the next tragedy occurs. If a room full of school children was swept away in Hurricane Sandy, Mayors Bloomberg and Emanuel would call for more gun control.

Sandy Hook Massacre

MOLON LABE!

I will not turn in my spade for a gift card; your bark doesn't intimidate me, I am not alone and let the resolve of millions of patriots with an understanding of history and firearms, give you pause. I pray to God that it won't come to it; but if tyranny comes to our doorstep it is most likely to come in uniform, at the dictate of rogue politicians and guarded by the propaganda of a dozen news anchors. What will you do? I can tell you how a "free man" would respond: a short prayer followed by two to the chest and one to the head; come what may!

May it never be! And it will be a lot less likely the more that Americans arm themselves. Arm yourselves in every way and make no apologies for it – ask a Holocaust Jew if he would, ask an Armenian.

Our Founders felt it necessary to include not only the protections to keep the citizen armed, but the injunction to keep him free:

We hold these truths to be self-evident, that all men are created equal, that they are endowed by their Creator with certain unalienable Rights, that among these are Life, Liberty and the pursuit of Happiness. – That to secure these rights, Governments are instituted among Men, deriving their just powers from the consent of the governed, — That whenever any Form of Government becomes destructive of these ends, it is the Right of the People to alter or to abolish it, and to institute new Government, laying its foundation on such principles and organizing its powers in such form, as to them shall seem most likely to effect their Safety and Happiness.

About the Author

John Kirkwood is a son of Issachar. He is a Zionist, gun-toting, cigar-smoking, incandescent light bulb-using, 3.2 gallon flushing, fur-wearing, Chinese (MSG) eating, bow-hunting, SUV driving, unhyphenated American man who loves his wife, isn't ashamed of his country and does not apologize for his Christianity. He Pastors Grace Gospel Fellowship Bensenville, where "we the people" seek to honor "In God we Trust." He hosts the Christian wake up call IN THE ARENA every Sunday at noon on AM 1160 and he co-hosts Un-Common Sense, the Christian Worldview with a double shot of espresso on UncommonShow.com. He is the proud homeschooling dad of Konnor, Karter and Payton and the "blessed from heaven above" husband of the Righteous and Rowdy Wendymae.

I suggest that we could some make positive change by not dismissing the heinous actions of bad men (and women) as "just crazy". What if the problem isn't the gun, the depression, the PTSD, or the bullying? What about the possibility that someone actually made a cruel choice... deliberately?

MASS SHOOTERS:
A PROBLEM OF PEOPLE, NOT GUNS

Written by Wes Walker

4 January 2013

Not much of an upgrade, is it – going from the "back of the bus" to beneath it? This past year, in headline after headline, that's exactly where people with mental illness have found themselves. We need to decide how we're going to treat them, because we can't have it both ways.

On the medical side, we take great pains to normalize mental illness. We want people to treat it like pneumonia, heart disease, or any other disorder: no shame and no stigma.

And then some idiot levels his gun at a crowd of innocents, and all that goes out the window. How can we hope to achieve that goal when we present mental illness as the catch-all explanation for every monstrous act of violence we see splashed across the news?

Does this sound familiar? "How could anyone do such a thing? What, he's got a mental illness? Well, that explains it."

With that one innocuous statement, they're all broad-brushed, and thrown under the bus. But it does NOT "explain it", any more than alcoholism "explains" drunk driving. Do we sneer at people from AA, thinking it's only a matter of time before they "snap", get bombed, and drive their car over a crossing guard?

No, we don't. Because that would be stupid. It would make two logical errors. First, that all drunk drivers are alcoholics. You don't have to be a chronic drinker to get behind the wheel after one too many. Second, it doesn't account for the alcoholics who never get behind the wheel after drinking, or those who dare not drink at all.

Violence works the same way. Are we really prepared to say that every lout that hurts (or worse) his wife and kids is mentally ill? That every schoolyard bully, gang-banger, terrorist, and mafioso who isn't constrained by conscience or compassion has a disorder? What about those whose illness never results in violence? Doesn't this attitude insult their character? Does it not reinforce the shame we're telling them not to feel?

Why the urgency to link killers like those in Oslo, Aurora, or Sandy Hook to mental illness? Probably because we see these actions as irrational behavior. If we can dismiss it as crazy, that's an answer we can deal with, and move on. If the guy's mind is broken, we don't have to understand it. It just "went wrong", and we can proceed to knee-jerk responses like awareness programs, disarming the public, or other superficial panaceas.

> *News flash: not all people with mental illness – even the violent sort – are the same. They are unique in all the ways that individuals always are.*

Some express their darker impulses by harming themselves (this varies from mild to extreme), but would take no interest in directing their energies outward. Others might smash property in a moment of unrestrained anger, but never lift a finger against a person. Still others may threaten, or cause physical harm to someone near them. In my line of work, I have seen each of these.

But I have also seen these seemingly-irrational outbursts overcome by introducing just a few changes into their lives. When a source of distress is identified, when circumstances are altered, when coping mechanisms are taught, and obviously (although it's usefulness is overstated) when medications are changed.

Most interesting to me, and relevant to this topic, is the process of discovering the "Function" of maladaptive behaviors. (These are: To avoid something, to gain something, to get attention, or for the direct enjoyment of the behavior itself.) Without the jargon: however irrational a specific behavior may seem, it is generally a means to some end. If you give that person a better way to achieve his goal – or provide a better goal to achieve – you will often see a change in that behavior.

Once you realize this, the "just crazy" excuse wears awfully thin. "Crazy people do crazy things" is what the headlines might tell us, and it might be easier to accept that the killer didn't really comprehend what he was doing.

That might even be accurate in some instances. But I have personally seen too many examples of seemingly irrational behavior interrupted by a clear and rational choice to blindly accept that blanket excuse.

I suggest that we could some make positive change by not dismissing the heinous actions of bad men (and women) as "just crazy". What if the problem isn't the gun, the depression, the PTSD, or the bullying? What about the possibility that someone actually made a cruel choice... deliberately?

Could we stop to consider that we live in a world where we are taught moral relativism, Nihilism, that man is merely a mammal, there is nothing after death, and nobody to give account to when we die? In such a world, why wouldn't some begin to live like there is no binding and objective Right and Wrong? (Neitzsche actually predicted this outcome.)

In the meantime, if we stop blaming mental illness for every heinous act we see, something good could come of this. Those who really do need help with mental illness might seek it.

And since stats tell us that one in four adults suffer from a diagnosable mental illness in a given year, don't we want those who really need help to get it?

ABOUT THE AUTHOR

Wes Walker is a Christian husband and father of three, bringing the Clash Attitude to Canada's Capital. When not writing submissions for Clash, he is involved in Church, his children's school, and is pursuing interests in Theology, History, and Philosophy.

Follow on twitter: @Republicanuck

Follow on Facebook at Wes.Walker.775.

Should the initial scenario present itself at my home, I intend to take that said person down; regardless of whether my husband is home or not. I am entitled to that and should be "allowed" to protect my home and my family as has been done throughout history.

Mom Sounds Off on Home Defense: Break into My House and I'll Kill You

Written By Mary Gjertsen

4 January 2013

It is 2:30 in the morning. Your small children are sound asleep in the room next to yours and the man of the house is working an overnight shift. As you lie in bed, you hear a shuffle outside your window. You quickly sit up as a large man crashes through that window and onto your bedroom floor. What do you do?

This is a scenario, along with many other similar stories, that we hear of far too frequently. In a society where threats are lurking around every corner, we cannot afford to allow our Second Amendment rights, our one source of protection, to be taken from us. Let me give you a little history lesson.

In 17th century England, it was a legal obligation that every household possess a gun to protect themselves. Yes, a legal obligation. Not a right. These individuals were not only responsible for protecting their homes, but were also accountable to their neighbors as well. On the American Frontier of the 18th century, every household owned a gun and every woman knew how to use this weapon. It was essential to the survival and protection of their families. There were even various states where it was a legal requirement that every capable member within a single household possess a gun. This became a vital source of protection during the American Revolution when many women were left to defend their property and their families while the men were away fighting for their freedom. There were no "gun free zones". These women stood their ground, legally and courageously. If there was even a minuscule chance that their lives were in danger, these incredible ladies had their guns by their sides; locked, loaded, and ready to aim with either a shotgun, pistol, or both.

Sandy Hook Massacre

As a wife, mother, and American citizen of this blessed nation, I take my Second Amendment rights very seriously. Should the initial scenario present itself at my home, I intend to take that said person down; regardless of whether my husband is home or not. I am entitled to that and should be "allowed" to protect my home and my family as has been done throughout history. Unfortunately, victims are now painted as the bad guy. This is a sham and insanity at its finest!

This country is quickly changing with all of the predicted gun laws and currently enacted gun free zones. Look at schools for example. If you do some research, you will find that there are a myriad of situations where an individual entered a school campus with the intent to harm. Coincidentally, you will find that a majority of these schools are also gun free zones. Will my daughters and son attend a school with a gun free zone? Absolutely not. Why? Because I don't want to hear of a dill weed, like ~~Name Deleted~~, waltzing into that school on a suicide mission and putting my child's life in danger; all for the sake of being politically acceptable.

Ladies and gentlemen, there is no better time than now to take a stand and make your voices heard. We cannot afford to be conveniently disarmed by a government that intends to control the very essence of whom we, the law abiding citizens, are and who we have worked so hard to become.

ABOUT THE AUTHOR

Mary is a stay-at-home mother of three beautiful kids and she heads up ClashChurch.com's children's ministry.

"This is a Remington 12 gauge pump action shotgun," I stated as boldly as I could muster. Right between the words gauge and pump I slammed the action open and closed. Let me tell you something, there are few things on this planet that get your attention more than that sound when it is unexpected.

I Took My Shotgun to High School

Written By SC Sherman

7 January 2013

One day back in 1987, I walked into High School carrying a 12 gauge shotgun. There was no fanfare. No shrieking, no lock down, and no one called 911. I didn't get arrested or go crazy. No one really cared. The biggest problem we had was trying to fit it into my locker. If I remember correctly, we made it work by placing my locker partner's trombone on top of the lockers just for that day. Just for the record and kudos … his name was Chris Shutts, currently serving in Afghanistan. Thanks Chris.

At this point you might wonder. How could this be? What would possess me to enter the hallowed halls of public school heavily armed? Why did no one react to protect the other stone-washed teens? Here's why. Guns were part of our lives.

Almost every guy I knew had a shotgun in his trunk or behind the seat of his truck. Why? Too many hours watching the original *Red Dawn*? No, it was in case we found something we wanted to shoot on the way to school of course. I'm not kidding. What if you were on your way to school and you spotted a beautiful ring-necked pheasant skulking through the ditch? Slam on the brakes; grab your trusty scattergun and bam, prairie chicken for dinner. One time on the way to school, I bagged a plump raccoon sitting on a snow drift. I think he might have waved at me, but that's another story. Raccoon's brought $30 back in the day.

I swaggered into school with my weapon for one reason alone. It was because I was deathly afraid to speak in public. No I'm not kidding. At Grinnell High School we were cruelly forced to give speeches up in front of our classmates. Sounds awful doesn't it? Well it was. This particular oration was to be the infamous "How to" speech, which means you had to teach your audience "How to" do something. Oh what to do? After agonizing over this for many hours I landed on my answer. How to give a "How to" speech and not puke on my classmates involved the one thing I was comfortable with, my shotgun.

I turned in an outline and Mr. Snyder approved it. "How to load a shotgun," by Steve Sherman. The awful day had come. I didn't just bring the gun to school, I brought the ammo too, probably eight shot, but I can't remember exactly. The time came for the actual speech. I was nervous. Beyond nervous, irrational fear gripped my mind. I thought of skipping out, but I didn't.

Sweat beaded on my forehead as I weaved down the halls with my books in one hand, my shotgun the other. I waited my turn as other people gave speeches on how to do laundry or how to bake really awesome cookies. I almost ruined my notes as I continued to frantically read over them. Suddenly, it was my turn. Back then, I didn't pray much, but I should have right then. It would have gone something like this: "Please God, I beg you don't let me look like an idiot. You know there are girls in this class, please help me!"

I stared back at my classmates as my throat had turned into the Mojave Desert. I unzipped my case and removed my old friend. The one thing I could count on other than my dog. I glanced at the teacher as he sat smiling behind his desk ready to grade my performance. I was ready. Mr. Snyder had said to have an "Attention Getter" at the beginning.

"This is a Remington 12 gauge pump action shotgun," I stated as boldly as I could muster. Right between the words gauge and pump I slammed the action open and closed. Let me tell you something, there are few things on this planet that get your attention more than that sound when it is unexpected.

I had a cheerleader in the front actually scream out and then bat her eyes a bit. I felt encouraged; this was going great! I kept going, my fears dissipated. I explained the safety, the sights, the recoil pad, and then I opened my box of shells and proceeded to demonstrate the proper loading technique, which of course culminates by slamming a shell into the chamber. I must admit there was an awkward pause at the end as I stood in front of my stunned class fully loaded. I was done. The speech didn't include unloading! I think I just said thank you and went to the corner of the room to unload.

I must say, it was one of the best speeches I ever gave. Both mullet-headed males and big-haired girls loved it! My teacher gave me an "A" and I lovingly put my shotgun back where it belonged, in my vehicle. We've always had lots of guns in America, at least in flyover country. We've even had guns in schools.

Our society is deteriorating before our eyes and we are trying to manage the decay. As a nation we could stand to remember who we are. Remember where we came from and what we are called to do as a people. We were once a great nation full of great people. I would submit that we still are, but we stand at the edge of an abyss much deeper than the fiscal cliff. Character, faith, honor, humility, and love, though out of fashion, still matter. We need resurgence in some of the old-school thinking. Will it happen? I don't know, but I'm going to teach it to my family. Maybe you will teach it to yours, too. That's a start.

I'm not sure what high school boys today would do a "How to" speech on. Maybe how to defeat a video game level or something? I have a sinking feeling that if one of my boys decided to give a speech like this today, he wouldn't get an "A" and afterwards we'd have to see him during visiting hours.

About the Author

S.C. Sherman grew up a farm kid in rural Iowa. He graduated from the University of Iowa with a degree in Communications Studies. Steve is a business owner, and recently ran for Iowa State House of Representatives.. S.C. enjoys political commentary and great stories. He has written three fiction novels found at www.scsherman.com He currently lives with his wife and four children in North Liberty, Iowa.

When and if hyper-inflation should happen, unfortunately, violent activities such as rape and shootings will also increase. I find it to be my responsibility to not only protect myself but my family.

THE GUN AS A CONSTANT COMPANION

Written By David Hiatt

7 January 2013

Firearms in America is hitting an all-time record thanks to Obama and his minions attempting to trash the Second Amendment and talk childishly about gun ammunition restrictions. Upon purchase of an additional firearm and ammunition this weekend, a photo of Barry and a caption said it all, "World's Greatest Gun Salesmen".

In December, 2,783,765 total background checks were made to purchase firearms, surpassing the previous record from November 2012 when 2,006,919 checks were performed. I believe January 2013 will surpass both November's and December's records. I frequent gun stores and just started going to shows when they are in the area. In the last few months there has been visible evidence that this government will not shut down those who enjoy and understand the importance of firearms. The shelves have been emptied of many types of rifles, specifically the AR-15 and other semi-automatic weapons with magazines that hold more than ten rounds.

The "Gun and Knife" show that I attended was extremely heavy with foot traffic and purchases. One would almost feel naked if leaving without a knife, pistol, rifle or shotgun. I did not see one AR at this event that was for sale. I must say it is a nice semi-automatic firearm and it would be a shame to see it and other rifles in the same class deemed illegal to own or purchase.

The FBI's National Instant Check System (NICS) requires only a few minutes for a gun purchase approval after completing the required form. Amazingly, less than 100 of these checks are denied nationally per year. After talking with local law enforcement officers in Indiana, I found that there is a four month wait due to the demand of "Concealed Carry Permits". The process can be started online and completed by visiting the County Police Department for the background check, additional paperwork and finger printing. Class III rifles and pistols (fully automatic firearms) take as long as six to seven months for approval and, yes, to this date they can still be purchased legally if you are willing to part with a big chunk of change.

Being a corn fed country boy, we always had guns on the farm as did most farmers in the community. The need for shooting a rabid fox or a family of groundhogs that fed off the planted field beans and corn was an annual occurrence. Just the sport of shooting cans off the fence was an event that created memorable family times.

Today, I believe more and more gun owners are not only making firearms purchases for sport but for self-preservation. Also as adults, we act much like children. If we are told that there is a possible chance we will no longer be able to have what we want, then the need for that want increases, ergo, we purchase what we may not be able to purchase in the future.

We haven't hit the so called "Fiscal Cliff" yet but when we do, it is only natural for home burglaries and theft to see an increase. When and if hyper-inflation should happen, unfortunately, violent activities such as rape and shootings will also increase. I find it to be my responsibility to not only protect myself but my family. None of us want to see this time come, but I believe it is only prudent to be prepared.

"A strong body makes the mind strong. As to the species of exercises, I advise the gun. While this gives moderate exercise to the body, it gives boldness, enterprise and independence to the mind. Games played with the ball and others of that nature, are too violent for the body and stamp no character on the mind. Let your gun therefore be the constant companion of your walks." — Thomas Jefferson

About the Author

David Hiatt sees a good part of America driving his truck across it, mostly from Indiana down to the bottom of Texas. He is a passionate Christian Constitutional Conservative that is concerned about the direction this Great Nation is heading.

... if you think for a second that Leftists are cool with hunting and Americans owning any type of firearms then you are definitely a few fries short of a Happy Meal.

CAN YOU IMAGINE KING GEORGE III TELLING OUR NATION'S FOUNDERS THEY COULDN'T HAVE MUSKETS?

Written By Doug Giles

7 January 2013

Don't you love how the Left and their step-n-fetch media mavens are trying to make law-abiding gun owners the bad guys? You don't? Yeah, me neither.

From Hollywood's heavily armed guarded elite to the radical, anti-gun commie rag *Journal News*, peaceful and upright average Joes are being isolated and concentrated on as the bane of America's existence just because we righteously and lawfully keep and bear arms.

Hollywood has even cobbled together a little tsk-tsk black and white video demanding our government do something about gun violence. That would be the very gun violence they have glamorized on the big screen for the last few decades. Hello.

I believe the total head count of the people slaughtered on film from all the participants from the "Demand a Plan" anti-gun clip comes out to a whopping 100,000 on-screen murders.

Yes, Hollywood, please lecture us about gun violence wrecking our culture. Life imitates art, morons, and your films probably spawned half of the killers' bloody dreams for the last two decades. Lecture us? Please. Physician, heal thyself.

Check it out: When upright, law-abiding Americans want your opinion on guns we'll give it to you, Hollyweird. Now, go back to Spago and suck on some edamame beans, you duplicitous little dandies.

Oh, and by the way, if you truly want to stem the tide of violent deaths, you should have made a video about the danger of hammers and clubs, as the FBI reports they kill more people every year than rifles do. Dorks.

You know what else is funny? The multitudinous politicians and pundits—mostly progressives—telling us what type of guns we should and should not own. "Oh, we shouldn't have semi-automatic weapons with thumb holes and extended mags," they say. "You should only have hunting guns," they opine.

First off, if you think for a second that Leftists are cool with hunting and Americans owning any type of firearms then you are definitely a few fries short of a Happy Meal.

These tree-humpers would have banned hunting and hunting guns yesterday if they had the wherewithal to do it. Secondly, the right to keep and bear arms was never about putting the bam to Bambi; it was always about the right to self-defense, especially against oppressive governments. Ah-hem.

Therefore, when a progressive tells you what kind of gun you should and shouldn't own, you should yawn and go out and buy what they just said you shouldn't have, like millions of other Americans have.

Finally, can you imagine if King George told our original rebels that they shouldn't own a musket? The Brown Bess, the Charleville and the Kentucky long rifle were the military/police weapons of the day, ladies and gents. "Yes, by George, you colonists shouldn't have a musket. Who needs a musket? You can hunt with a bow and arrow or a slingshot or a snare. No one needs a dangerous musket. We have the muskets, and we'll protect you … maybe."

Our founding rebels with a cause would have said (did say), "Yeah, thanks, but no thanks, Georgie Boy. We'll leave our self-defense to ourselves. Now bugger off, you snaggle-toothed oppressor, and don't make me use this."

Oh, one last thing: Here's a little history lesson regarding gun-grabbing and the carnage that ensued:

In 1929, the Soviet Union established gun control. From 1929 to 1953, about 20 million dissidents, unable to defend themselves, were rounded up and exterminated.

In 1911, Turkey established gun control. From 1915 to 1917, 1.5 million Armenians, unable to defend themselves, were rounded up and exterminated.

Germany established gun control in 1938 and from 1939 to 1945, a total of 13 million Jews and others who were unable to defend themselves were rounded up and exterminated.

China established gun control in 1935. From 1948 to 1952, 20 million political dissidents, unable to defend themselves were rounded up and exterminated.

Guatemala established gun control in 1964. From 1964 to 1981, 100,000 Mayan Indians, unable to defend themselves, were rounded up and exterminated.

Uganda established gun control in 1970. From 1971 to 1979, 300,000 Christians, unable to defend themselves, were rounded up and exterminated.

Cambodia established gun control in 1956. From 1975 to 1977, one million educated people, unable to defend themselves, were rounded up and exterminated.

Defenseless people rounded up and exterminated in the 20th century because of gun control: 56 million.

You won't see this data on the U.S. evening news or hear politicians disseminating this information. Guns in the hands of honest citizens save lives and property and, yes, gun-control laws adversely affect only the law-abiding citizens.

ABOUT DOUG GILES

Doug Giles is the man behind ClashDaily.com. In addition to driving ClashDaily.com, Giles is a popular columnist on Townhall.com and the author of the book Raising Righteous & Rowdy Girls.

Doug's articles have also appeared on several other print and online news sources, including The Washington Times, The Daily Caller, Fox Nation, USA Today, The Wall Street Journal, The Washington Examiner, The Blaze, American Hunter Magazine and ABC News.

He's been a frequent guest on the Fox News Channel and Fox Business Channel as well as many nationally syndicated radio shows across the nation — which, he believes, officially makes him a super hero.

In addition, Doug is an occasional guest host on New York City's WABC (The Jason Mattera Show) and he is a weekly guest, every Friday at 7:45am[et], on America's Morning News (155 markets).

Giles and his wife Margaret have two daughters: Hannah, who devastated ACORN with her 2009 nation shaking undercover videos, and Regis who is an NRA columnist, huntress and Second Amendment activist.

DG's interests include guns, big game hunting, big game fishing, fine art, cigars, helping wounded warriors, and being a big pain in the butt to people who dislike God and the USA.

Read more Doug Giles at www.clashdaily.com.

More regulations, special taxes, outright bans, and the flushing of the Second Amendment down the Congressional toilet will not solve the crisis we face. It will, of course, give the government a big fat pat on the back, a reason to celebrate. The same government that swears to uphold the Constitution. The irony shouldn't be lost on anyone.

Chicago is #1

Written by Pauline Wolak

9 January 2013

First and last name; check. Address; check. Are you a US citizen? Yes and check. Date of birth, social security number, signature; check, check and check! Height, weight, gender, hair color. Whew, this application is getting pretty detailed! Thank you for the checklist, Illinois. I nearly forgot to include my photo and $10 fee. And voila, I am now registered for my Illinois Voter ID Card.

Just kidding! It's actually an application for a "firearms owner's identification card." All Illinoisans must apply for said card before they can legally own a firearm. ANY firearm, not just the oft (and erroneously) feared handgun or "assault rifle." About 1.4 million people in Illinois have a FOID card. 1.4 million times 10... Let's just assume the state of Illinois had about 14,000,000 to start the FOID program in 1968.

Between FOID rules, the ban on concealed carry permits, and the Chicago handgun ban, it's no wonder Chicago is so free of crime. Wait. What's that you say? Chicago's murder rate went UP last year? Nooooo. It can't be.

So much for community organizing.

It never ceases to amaze me. Illinois actually charges law-abiding citizens a $10 fee to carry a worthless piece of paper. Meanwhile, in Chicago, 506 murders occurred last year. A vast majority of those murders occurred with a firearm. How many were with legally obtained and owned firearms, you ask? Who knows? Only about 25% of those homicides were even solved. The first 8 days of this year Chicago has already seen 12 murders. That'll put them on pace to, once again, earn the crown of America's deadliest city.

Sandy Hook Massacre

How are all of those gun laws working out for you, Chicago?

It doesn't take a rocket scientist to understand that all the laws in the world aren't going to stop a criminal. Since Sandy Hook I have heard the argument that the shooter was able to obtain weapons and that's why we need stricter laws. Never mind that he committed murder to get to the weapons. He then stole the weapons, since he was too young to purchase his own legally in the state of Connecticut. It shouldn't be lost on anyone he also went on his shooting rampage in a "gun free zone." Law upon law upon law. Not one of them stopped a criminal hell bent on destruction.

The same goes for Chicago. Banning concealed weapons certainly didn't help Terrence Wright, 18, who was fatally shot during a robbery last year. It didn't help 25 year-old David Kartzmark who was murdered just last week.

Gangs, the breakdown of the family, poverty, lack of education; these are the things that ill cities like Chicago. And all the gun bans in the world aren't going to solve the problem. When will we begin the discussion that really needs to happen? The one that addresses our dwindling belief in traditional family values. The one that asks why 8 year-old boys need to play violent video games. The one that begins to sort out the mess that our mental health system has become. The one that asks Hollywood why it doesn't feel guilty for making billions on gratuitously violent movies and television shows.

More regulations, special taxes, outright bans, and the flushing of the Second Amendment down the Congressional toilet will not solve the crisis we face. It will, of course, give the government a big fat pat on the back, a reason to celebrate. The same government that swears to uphold the Constitution. The irony shouldn't be lost on anyone.

Michael Steele summed it up well. *"You can have all the gun control laws in the country, but if you don't enforce them, people are going to find a way to protect themselves. We need to recognize that bad people are doing bad things with these weapons. It's not the law-abiding citizens, it's not the person who uses it as a hobby."* Criminals are going to get weapons. It's a fact. Putting up barriers to legally obtain a gun will just make more victims, not less.

I believe Clint Eastwood said it best, though. "I have a very strict gun control policy: if there's a gun around, I want to be in control of it."

About the Author

Pauline is a proud stay-at-home wife and mother of three. By "at home" she means everywhere but home. She spends her time volunteering for various projects and charities as well as being "that mom" on the PTO and school board. After her family, she lives for coffee, football, and sharing her opinion with anyone that will (and sometimes won't) listen! She's an unabashed pro-life Catholic. Please follow her on Twitter at https://twitter.com/MiStateFan or visit clashdaily.com.

To "keep" and "bear" arms means, per SCOTUS, to have weapons and to carry weapons. So this decision protects the individual's right to own and carry weapons, period.

SCOTUS AND GUN CONTROL, PART I

Written by Suzanne Olden

9 January 2013

There have been two decisions handed down by the Supreme Court of the United States ("SCOTUS") in the last four years about the Second Amendment. I am going to discuss both and how they could affect any attempt to legislate away that important right. The first is District of Columbia v. Heller, 128 S. Ct. 2783 (2008). This decision is going to be very important in crafting or fighting any legislation that should come out from Obama's commission on the subject, as it deals with an outright ban on handguns.

D.C. law prohibited the possession of handguns, registration of handguns, and required that lawfully owned firearms (not handguns), "unloaded and dissembled or bound by a trigger lock or similar device". Dick Heller, was a D.C. special police officer and carried a handgun while on duty at the Federal Judicial Center. When he applied to register it to keep at home, he was turned down.

As we are all well aware, the Second Amendment says: *"A well regulated Militia, being necessary to the security of a free State, the right of the people to keep and bear Arms, shall not be infringed."* Seems simple enough, but this case has two very different views about those words. One side believes that only the right to possess and carry a firearm in connection with militia service is protected. The other that it protects an individual right to possess a firearm, and use of the firearm is for traditionally lawful purposes, such as defending your home and family. SCOTUS agreed with the latter and defends its majority position in two ways: first, through looking at the actual language of the Amendment, and second through its history.

The Second Amendment says the "right of the people." This is important in that it is used in only two other places in the Constitution, the First and Fourth Amendments. Neither of them refer to "group" rights, but individual ones. While this contrasts with the reference to militia in the beginning of the Amendment, the history and understanding of the people of the time will show that individuals, not militias, are the protected class. SCOTUS rightfully started with the presumption that the Second Amendment right is exercised individually and belongs to all Americans.

"Arms" have a specific meaning as well. There have been arguments that either it means only those to be used for the military (which they would then ban for citizens, effectively banning all firearms) or that it applied to only arms in existence in the 18th century. The legal definition, now and at the time of the Founding Fathers, was that "arms" were not specifically weapons designed for military use. The court called this last argument applying to only 18th century arms as "frivolous." Other rights protected by the Constitution, like the First and Fourth Amendments have been stretched to apply to modern America and technology, as should the Second.

To "keep" and "bear" arms means, per SCOTUS, to have weapons and to carry weapons. So this decision protects the individual's right to own and carry weapons, period.

History more than adequately shows the intent of the Framers, and the understanding of the populace at the time. Since our law largely derived from English law, SCOTUS had to look no further than English history. One argument made by gun rights advocates is that disarming the populace is the easiest way to take them over, and history does bear that out. Kings Charles II and James II were highly successful in using militias loyal to them to suppress political dissidents. They also suppressed their Protestant opponents by outlawing their ownership of arms. Because of this, the English Bill of Rights specifically stated that Protestants would never be disarmed.

That didn't stop George III from trying to do the same to the colonists. In the 1760's and 1770's, he began to disarm the colonists. Obviously that didn't go well, as the colonists knew their rights as English subjects. In fact, the debate about the Second Amendment didn't center around whether individuals should be able to own arms. That was a given. To quote SCOTUS: "During the 1788 ratification debates, the fear that the federal government would disarm the people in order to impose rule through a standing army or select militia was pervasive..." History does tend to repeat itself.

Moving forward in history, before the Civil War, Antislavery advocates routinely invoked the right to bear arms for self-defense. Afterwards, Blacks were routinely disarmed by Southern States. A Congressional report from the time said: "in some parts of [South Carolina], armed parties are, without proper authority, engaged in seizing all fire-arms found in the hands of the freemen. Such conduct is in clear and direct violation of their personal rights as guaranteed by the Constitution of the United States, which declares that `the right of the people to keep and bear arms shall not be infringed.' The freedmen of South Carolina have shown by their peaceful and orderly conduct that they can safely be trusted with fire-arms, and they need them to kill game for subsistence, and to protect their crops from destruction by birds and animals." Joint Comm. on Reconstruction, H.R.Rep. No. 30, 39th Cong., 1st Sess., pt. 2, p. 229 (1866)

The Court even addressed the issue of banning some guns over others. They stated that the D.C. assertion that banning handguns is ok because long guns are permissible is not a solution. They noted that for various good reasons, Americans have long considered the handgun to be the quintessential self-defense weapon, and that the complete prohibition of handguns is invalid.

Bottom line is this: SCOTUS held that "the District's ban on handgun possession in the home violates the Second Amendment, as does its prohibition against rendering any lawful firearm in the home inoperable for the purpose of immediate self-defense…" Banning ownership is unconstitutional. Requiring guns to be in pieces or trigger locked is unconstitutional.

About the Author

Suzanne Reisig Olden is a Catholic Christian, Conservative, married mother of two. She lives northwest of Baltimore, in Carroll County, Maryland. She graduated of Villa Julie College/Stevenson University with a BS in Paralegal Studies and works as a paralegal for a franchise company, specializing in franchise law and intellectual property. Originally from Baltimore, and after many moves, she came home to raise her son and daughter, now ages 17 and 13, in her home state. Suzanne also writes for the online publication, *The Beacon Bulletin*.

Read more of her work at http://beaconbulletin.com/.

Unfortunately, for the tragic victims of Newtown, Connecticut, the government in Washington, has decided to disarm its citizens by using the very laws that Hancock and other Founding Fathers fought so desperately for.

THE SECOND WAR OF INDEPENDENCE IS DECLARED

Written By Kevin Fobbs

10 January 2013

There is a sickening aroma in the air that is beginning to permeate the very soul of independent, freedom embracing Americans. It began to originate long before the shooting at Aurora, Colorado, or recently in Newtown, Connecticut. Its rancid fragrance seeps into the fabric of the U.S. Constitution and is emitted by the control terrorists who manipulate the facts and perceptions of Americans who watch the news. These purveyors of stricter gun control measures seek to erode your defenses so that in your weakened state you will accept their sweet smelling tyranny.

The nation that was represented as a symbolic shining city on a hill that President Ronald Reagan spoke about over 30 years ago, is now becoming a broken mud hole of shattered dreams. America's morning that has dawned over the nation is now bearing witness to the shredding of constitutional protections which have safe guarded families since the infancy of the republic. Obama has given the order to Vice President Biden: full steam ahead to obliterate gun rights to your town. You and your family are the targets and what will you do?

The reaction by gun owners and even prospective gun owners to Obama's desperate zeal is to hurry up and buy up all the potential guns and now-legal weapons that might be taken by edict or by force by the government. That may be a solution, but it is only a temporary one.

Once the federal government has quenched its thirst on stripping away gun rights, it will not hesitate to take the next step to criminalize actual possession of banned weapons!

Then what will you do? What is the response to a government that embraces tyrannical rule over the constitutional guarantees and protections contained within the U.S. Constitution? What are you, the father, the mother, the son or the daughter prepared to do when, the government official, acting on direct orders from a new commission set up by President Obama to confiscate your guns, knocks at your door?

Where are the defenders of the U.S. Constitution who are elected in Congress? Are you absolutely certain they will not give in, and knuckle under Obama's determination which is aided by the mainstream media talking heads? Remember these are the same talking heads that avoided Obama's dismissive behavior in not enforcing congressional legislation. This is the same mainstream media that buried the White House Benghazi murder cover up as if it never happened. Think about your choices when seeking to rely upon the fourth estate which has been rendered a useless patsy for the Obama administration.

Now, do you really believe that once your guns are banned, and the weapons that were grandfathered, will not be taken in the second round of gun control legislation?

The War for Independence initially began with a flurry of gunshots which rang out in Boston on March 5, 1770, and there Americans drew the line in the sand against British imperialism and tyranny. The first to die, Crispus Attucks, a Blackman, and the twenty others with him had sticks and clubs, and the British soldiers had guns. Obviously sticks and clubs were no match, then nor are they now.

John Hancock, one of the nation's Founding Fathers spoke of that legendary heroic moment, by urging, *"for a well-regulated militia of the whole people who would fight "for their liberty, and for themselves, and for their God."*

Unfortunately, for the tragic victims of Newtown, Connecticut, the government in Washington, has decided to disarm its citizens by using the very laws that Hancock and other Founding Fathers fought so desperately for. Instead, Obama, Biden and gun control mayors like New York City's Michael Bloomberg, continuously assault the U.S. Constitutional Second Amendment rights. They work to manipulate this tragedy to lead a sustained assault on freedom of defense against tyranny.

The goal of the gun-control activists is clear. They use their partnership with the mainstream media to paint a portrait of tragedy across the television screens of America's living rooms and blame guns as the cause. They seek to nurture, cajole, neutralize or tempt Americans with the notion that guns created the havoc, and misery and tragedy that befell the victims.

The victimizers who pulled the trigger and who designed the loathsome events are never held to account for any responsibility in perpetrating the heinous deeds. The incredulousness of this rationale defines logic. Taken to a logical conclusion, you would have to think the gun actually forced the assassins to pick up the weapon and pull the trigger.

America, if you fall victim to this criminalization of your own legal rights, then the forces of Obama and his socialist tyranny have already won half of the battle.

These next few weeks, should not just be a wait-and-see-what-will-happen-in-Washington-D.C. interval. This has to be a time where you, the defender of your house, your home, your castle, embrace the belief that true representation begins in your home, not in Washington, D.C.

Each American must first determine for yourself, that you are ready to speak to your neighbor, your family member, your co-worker, or your friend, and ask, "What are you prepared to do, to hold your congressman or woman responsible?"

The congress cannot pass a law unless both houses pass the legislation to begin stripping your rights and the President signs it. If Obama tries to use an executive order to do it, then demand it be overridden and demonstrate until it is overridden!

The Second War of Independence is not when you begin to see the Obama gun control brigade at your door, it begins when you decide to do nothing, and just let it happen.

About the Author

Kevin Fobbs has more than 35 years of wide-ranging experience as a community and tenant organizer, Legal Services outreach program director, public relations consultant, business executive, gubernatorial and presidential appointee, political advisor, widely published writer, and national lecturer. Kevin is co-chair and co-founder of AC-3 (American-Canadian Conservative Coalition) that focuses on issues on both sides of the border between the two countries.

Let there be no mistake. They have always wanted our guns, because it's not about guns; it's about control. Vladimir Lenin said, "One man with a gun can control 100 without one. ... Make mass searches and hold executions for found arms."

The Second Amendment is the Nuclear Option

Written By Skip Coryell

10 January 2013

The year was nineteen-sixty-two. The President was John F. Kennedy. The Cuban missile crisis began on 15 October and continued on for thirteen days after an American U2 aircraft took photographs of missile sites under construction on the communist island of Cuba. The Soviet Union was about to place medium-range and intermediate-range ballistic nuclear missiles just ninety-four miles off the Florida Keys. It is generally regarded as the closest the world has ever come to total annihilation.

For thirteen tense days the world balanced on the apex of the knife. Fall to the left – we die. Fall to the right – we're enslaved. President Kennedy didn't flinch. Premier Khrushchev backed down and nuclear war was averted. But the strategy of Mutual Assured Destruction (MAD) was born.

Fast forward to January 9, 2013. Vice President Joe Biden bangs his shoe on the table and says:

"The president is going to act … There are executive orders, there's executive action that can be taken. We haven't decided what that is yet. But we're compiling it all with the help of the attorney general and the rest of the cabinet members as well as legislative action that we believe is required."

The Second Amendment is now under attack like never before. Joe Biden's words were the proverbial "shot across the bow" as a precursor to all-out war on American gun owners. Have the anti-gunners overstepped? Or, will they succeed in killing American freedom for generations to come?

Isn't that up to us, the American people? And hasn't it always been so? We are at a crossroads in history, and we can choose to buy peace at the price of chains and slavery, or we can stand up and fight for the liberty of our children and our children's children. There's a lot at stake.

What the Obama administration is proposing is nothing short of MAD. It's the Cuban Missile Crisis of our generation, and how we respond to it will define us. Yet they seem so cock-sure, so confident that it's unnerving. But arrogance is a weakness that cries out for exploitation. I say we give it to them. If this is a trial balloon, then we blow it out of the sky, thereby sending them a message once and forever that Americans will not go quietly into the night. We will not bow and accept the noose. Instead, if you come to take our guns, then we will fight. The phrase "Molon Labe" (come and get them) has never been more relevant.

Let there be no mistake. They have always wanted our guns, because it's not about guns; it's about control. Vladimir Lenin said, "One man with a gun can control 100 without one. ... Make mass searches and hold executions for found arms."

The Vice President has told us this is a moral issue and that "it's critically important that we act."

He's right. It is a moral issue. It is important we act.

The only reason the strategy of Mutual Assured Destruction worked is because both sides believed the other would retaliate with deadly force. The same is true for us. The anti-gunners have been held at bay only because of the real threat of bloody revolution should the government come to take our guns. As long as the government believes we'll revolt, they'll minimize their tyranny. But the moment they think we'll flinch, then it's Katy bar the door, because the ATF will be kicking down doors all over America like the jack-booted thugs they are.

The Vice President called for responsible action. "If your actions result in only saving one life, they're worth taking. But I'm convinced we can affect the well-being of millions of Americans and take thousands of people out of harm's way if we act responsibly."

He's right. He has the power to save millions of Americans on both sides by taking responsible action. All he has to do is back down. But he'll never do that if gun owners don't stand firm, shoulder-to-shoulder, united against tyranny. If you've been sitting on the fence letting others do the work for you, now is the time to step up and let your voices be heard. Because if you don't, if we don't blow that trial balloon out the sky and fast, then we'll find ourselves and our sons and daughters knee-deep in American blood and a shooting war.

The Second Amendment is the nuclear option of our day, and it can't be taken off the table. If it is, if Americans don't have the nerve or will to fight against tyranny; if they bend the knee and kiss the ring of a tyrant, we will be enslaved forever. Learn the lessons of English gun owners. It's much easier to defend a hill you own than to retake it after it's been surrendered. Defend the hill of freedom. If it comes to a fight, then, so be it. Some of us will die. But until then scream bloody murder. Because the Second Amendment is a hill worth living for and, if necessary, dying to defend.

About the Author

Skip Coryell lives with his wife and children in Michigan. Skip Coryell is the author of nine books including *Blood in the Streets: Concealed Carry and the OK Corral*, *RKBA: Defending the Right to Keep and Bear Arms*, *The God Virus*, and *We Hold These Truths*. He is the founder of The Second Amendment March, a Marine Corps veteran, and the President of White Feather Press. He is an avid hunter and sportsman, a Marine Corps veteran, and a graduate of Cornerstone University. For more details on Skip Coryell, or to contact him personally, go to his website at skipcoryell.com

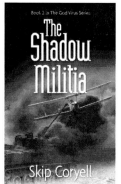

To get a copy of Skip's latest novel *The Shadow Militia*, go to store.whitefeatherpress.com or amazon. com.

Could it be — just asking — that for the Second-Amendment spurning mainstream media the non-Sandy Hook killings don't square sufficiently with their anti-firearm agenda? Perhaps, even less permissibly, contain elements that jam up their gun-grabbing narrative?

POST NEWTOWN: TIME TO JUST BAN EVERYTHING?

Written By Steve Pauwels

10 January 2013

Perhaps the Christmas 2012 season was bloodier than normal — or perhaps December 14th's particularly heinous Sandy Hook elementary school massacre in suburban Newtown, Connecticut only makes it seem so. In any case, lots of people died violently over several pre-holiday weeks. And, adding to the awfulness, the widespread reaction has been an exasperatingly predictable exercise in distraction and misdirection.

Actually, to clarify: it's the reaction to the Connecticut atrocity that's been vocally wrongheaded. December's other outbreaks of firearms carnage have, by comparison, been forgotten pretty quickly by the national press and commentariat.

In case you don't know, three days preceding Sandy Hook's slaughter of a score of pre-adolescents and handful of school personnel, an amply armed Oregon man walked into a Portland shopping mall and opened fire, killing two and wounding a third before taking his own life.

Exactly one week after the Newtown mayhem, Jeffrey Lee Michael launched a central Pennsylvania killing spree, taking the lives of three civilians and injuring a trio of State Troopers before they finally shot him dead. Days later — Christmas Eve morning — a 62 year old ex-con cut down four Webster, NY firefighters who responded when he set his own home ablaze; two subsequently died. As the inferno spread through his neighborhood, the shooter, William Spengler, Jr., was pinned down by an arriving policeman before dying himself from a self-inflicted gunshot wound.

It's certainly understandable why Sandy Hook's nightmare has garnered the gruesome lion's share of attention: weeks later, photos of its angelic victims, never mind the heart-rending accounts of helpless school officials sacrificing their lives protecting the children, continue to mesmerize. Still, it's not like these other depravities are exactly run-of-the-mill: holiday shoppers targeted in Oregon? A shoot-out with PA State Police following the execution of, among others, a woman who'd been innocently decorating a church? A Christmas Eve crossfire, complete with a literal conflagration and the slaying of devoted public servants? Not exactly the yawn-inducing stuff of "just another" news cycle; but nearly disregarded when contrasted to the school shooting focus.

Could it be — just asking — that for the Second-Amendment spurning mainstream media the non-Sandy Hook killings don't square sufficiently with their anti-firearm agenda? Perhaps, even less permissibly, contain elements that jam up their gun-grabbing narrative?

In the Oregon mall pandemonium, for instance, a masked, AR-15-toting Jacob Tyler Roberts was halted, in part, when bystander Nick Meli confronted him with his own Glock 22. Notice: whereas the villain used a firearm — one he'd stolen the day before, by the way — to wreak sanguinary havoc, the good guy used his to stymie it, likely diminishing the body count in the process. In this scenario, guns weren't only part of the problem, but played a role in its solution — dismaying, no doubt, the "firearms-are-the-devil" set.

Ban guns because Sandy Hook's shooter (Name removed by the publisher and shall hereafter be referred to as 'He who shall not be named.') employed them to horrific ends? Just like December 21st's Pennsylvania perpetrator? Then, perhaps motor vehicles should be outlawed as well — since the Keystone State killer also assaulted two of his victims with his pick-up truck. Though not widely reported, in the course of his rampage Jeffrey Lee Michael rammed head-on into not only a car, but a state trooper's cruiser, as well.

A firearm was misused. So, too, a motor vehicle. The only solution? It must be to make them both across-the-board illegal, right?

Except that — slightly complicating this tidy deduction — it turns out an off-duty cop attempted to protect the fallen firefighters with his car; an action Webster Police Chief Gerald Pickering praised as "heroic".

Hmm — motor vehicle as instrument of evil and of heroism? It's all so very confusing. Maybe we should just stick with the former.

Which, inevitably, prompts the question: at what point do all these "banning" proposals overreach?

People abuse bladed tools all the time — is it time for knives to be removed from general circulation? Racial-radio-huckster Al Sharpton recently suggested as much: "What happens when the criminal goes to knives … ?" a December 28 caller asked the talk host.

"Then you deal with knives," Sharpton replied. "The job of society is to deal with whatever problem confronts it."

For the record, Sharpton's not alone in these anti-cutlery cogitations: the UK's BBC is reporting that a team of "Accident and Emergency" doctors is decrying the availability of intolerably long "domestic knives" — i.e., kitchenware. Shorter blades? They should still get the nod. Not their lengthier brethren, however — time for a ban in Britain!

Thus, ixnay on the: Guns. Cars. Knives. Anything else?

Since you ask: why not matches? Accelerants?

Recall, Webster, NY's Spengler fiendishly lured those first-responders into his ambush by staging a raging inferno. Not only did two end up dead and three more wounded, but seven homes were consumed. What was his fuel of choice? Kerosene? Acetone?

Furthermore, in an especially macabre twist, this is the second Christmas season in a row the Rochester suburb has experienced fire-related violence: in December 2011 a 15-year-old boy set his gasoline-doused house afire, killing his father and two brothers and injuring his mother and sister.

Which settles it: whatever their utility, flame and fuel have gotta go — must get to work on that!

Meanwhile, what goes unaddressed? Matters like: a feckless, pasta-spined court system which paroled Spengler in 1998, after his serving a paltry seventeen years for the pummeling death of his grandmother. Free, thereafter, to blissfully ignore his state's well-meaning, but too often irrelevant, gun-control restrictions, he burned down his block and gunned down brave men.

Matters like: The Oregon mall-shooter's similar flouting of firearms law on the way to transgressing yet others. (Criminals have a disconcerting, if reliable, habit of conducting themselves that way.)

Matters like: the beneficial service honorable citizens — law-enforcement or layman — can render society when they're at liberty to "keep and bear arms", (our Founders' phrasing).

Finally shunted aside is the notion that a principled community shouldn't punish responsible folks by denying them access to the worthwhile rights ill-used by irresponsible and wicked folks. Currently, that's a perspective not much abided, even though, not that long ago it was the popularly accepted one.

But that was before common sense was banned.

ABOUT THE AUTHOR

Steve Pauwels is managing editor of ClashDaily.com

Protesters camped on the disputed land. Injunctions were filed, but they didn't move. Next were roadblocks, burning tires, injuries to local homeowners — some were life-threatening — and damage to both public and private property on and around the affected land. The Provincial government proved itself unwilling and/or unable to protect the property and safety of private citizens impacted by the dispute.

Second Amendment: Do Militias Matter Today?

Written By Wes Walker

11 January 2013

The role of gun ownership has always been emotionally charged, but Sandy Hook's news has again heightened the rhetoric. This debate has spilled over and has become international.

Anti-gun lobbyists consider the Second Amendment antiquated, asking what militias could protect us from today. The pro-gun side answers: "Tyrants", citing King George III, Hitler's Germany, or another event so seemingly distant that the argument seems academic. Even some who want stricter controls might concede the home-defense argument. But they would never want Joe Public armed with the sorts of guns carried by soldiers and police. Are militias relevant today?

Do you think it strange that citizens might be called to grab their gun, and rush to the defense of their community or region against some threat? Why is it strange? Small towns do the same thing with volunteer fire departments. Bankers, plumbers, or gym teachers, all become firemen when there's a fire raging. You can't wait for experts to put out the fire, everybody gets involved. That same principle describes a militia.

The relevant Amendment reads: "A well regulated militia, being necessary to the security of a free state, the right of the people to keep and bear arms shall not be infringed."

This week, I stumbled on a modern, local parallel to this principle. A judge was complaining about a Provincial police force refusing to administer a court order. Reading further, I saw the connection.

Now, I need to proceed carefully. The example I'm citing is complex, and explosive. I could not possibly give the nuanced description that fairness would require. Others can debate who is right and wrong in the issue itself, I am only presenting a modern example of one effective application of the principles the Amendment defends.

Remember the taunt, "You and what army?" That's a defiant reply given when someone tries to force his will on you. It is also the response to tyranny embedded in the Second Amendment. A lone man could shoot a prowler in defense of his family. But this other use requires a group standing together, bearing arms against a threat — its own government, if need be — in mutual defense.

Today, not every group sees government as benign. For historical reasons, some doubt their motives and promises, old agreements remain disputed, and past wrongs color present-day relations.

That's why some Canadian Aboriginal groups have chosen to provide for their own protection. This is seen in periodic shows of force defying government edicts. Roads or railways are blockaded. (This was the case with Judge David Brown's injunction for Ontario Police to remove a railway barricade -- which police ignored.) We have had crises with names like Oka, or Caledonia, in which protesters make it clear they are prepared to use force to achieve their aims.

The Caledonia case is interesting. In 2006, protesters from Six Nations disputed the legality of an 1840's transaction relating to land now being developed. Protesters camped on the disputed land. Injunctions were filed, but they didn't move. Next were roadblocks, burning tires, injuries to local homeowners — some were life-threatening — and damage to both public and private property on and around the affected land. The Provincial government proved itself unwilling and/or unable to protect the property and safety of private citizens impacted by the dispute.

Unable to resolve the matter, the Province paid tens of millions in damages to the property owners/developers, millions more to the local businesses and residents, not to mention payouts to Dana Chatwell and Dave Brown (Google their story) and others. In 2013, this matter is still not resolved, yet is largely forgotten by the public.

Obviously, there are underlying grievances, precedents, racial tensions etcetera, beyond the scope of this brief description of the events to consider. But on a basic level, we see how one group that began what they would consider a peaceful protest calling attention to what they considered their lawful rights. Because they rejected court rulings against them as non-binding and invalid (it's complicated), they used strength of numbers, and sometimes physical force, to defy them.

Ethical considerations, and treatment of innocent civilians aside, this tactic was sufficiently effective that law enforcement did not — could not — force compliance on Six Nations protesters.

Contrast that to the disorganized, unarmed citizens of Caledonia, including but not limited to Dave Brown (arrested for "trespassing" on his own land), and "The Caledonia 8" (arrested without charge for wanting to walk down a street with a protest sign in August 2012). Locals even tried forming a militia (in 2009) to protect the interests their law enforcement wouldn't, but this was unsuccessful.

This is obviously an imperfect analogy to militias — especially because militias would typically defend their community, rather than displacing their neighbors. But strictly as a deterrent to the government use of force, this example of a group too willing and able to defend its interests forced government officials to change their tactics. Locals allege that government and law enforcement began using "kid gloves" in their dealings with Six Nations, but not with other Caledonians.

Suppose we find ourselves facing a government flagrantly abusing police powers over its citizens. Which of these groups will sleep soundly at night?

The moral of the story is this: Armed citizens are able to protect their rights, whether or not their governments acknowledge them.

About the Author

Wes Walker is a Christian husband and father of three, bringing the Clash Attitude to Canada's Capital. When not writing submissions for Clash, he is involved in Church, his children's school, and is pursuing interests in Theology, History, and Philosophy.

Follow on twitter: @Republicanuck

Follow on Facebook at Wes.Walker.775.

When we turned away from God and our morality, we turned away from self-government. The whole idea of a free nation was that people were moral enough to govern themselves.

Sex, Drugs and Lock n' Load

Written By Mark Mayberry

11 January 2013

As a so-called "millennial", I have a first hand view of what young adults and teenagers are seeing and doing in our post-religious society. In America we have thrown off the "chains" of religious tyranny; but in doing so what have we exchanged it for? In the wake of mass shootings and unimaginable death we come together as a society and demand answers to a problem that we have ourselves created. When you demand a Godless society be prepared to live in a lawless world.

At twenty-seven years of age I am old enough to remember prayer in my local elementary school and saying the pledge of allegiance without fear of offending someone. However, this generation has now become the generation of fatherless children and soulless individuals who think or care little for others and feel as though everything is permitted.

We put a lot of stock in our Founding Fathers as Americans and so, when I began this intellectual quest to answer the question as to why people are killing scores of people for no reason, I started with John Adams. Adams said, "Our constitution was made only for a moral and religious people. It is wholly inadequate to the government of any other." When we turned away from God and our morality, we turned away from self-government. The whole idea of a free nation was that people were moral enough to govern themselves.

The real truth is that guns are not dooming our society, we are. Kids today are bombarded by a toxic flood of death, sex and drugs from the time they are old enough to turn on the television. We tell our children that there is no judgment and no God to answer to and then we sit in awe when a twenty year old kills twenty-six people, twenty of them children, right before Christmas. We have replaced God with self and now instead of facing the facts, we would rather blame inanimate objects than ourselves.

There have been school shootings since the beginning of our great nation. However before 1989 there were but a handful of mass killings in our schools. But after 1989 there were forty such occurrences. We find all kinds of reasons as to why these things happen; people are crazy, kids play violent video games, guns are too easy to get and so on. But how can we expect anything less in a world where we freely accept people who are governed by their own hedonistic desires and where drugs and alcohol flood our streets like open sewers.

To pretend like we can legislate away our broken moral compass is to pretend that we can put out a fire by simply ignoring it. Guns have been a part of American culture since the beginning. George Washington famously said a free people ought to be armed. Are we still a free people? This new age of political correctness we live in is nothing more than tyranny with manners according to the late Charlton Heston. Along with this political correctness has come this idea that we cannot judge another person based upon the morality of their actions.

An immoral and Godless people have no problem killing each other. This is the real issue. Many of the same people who fed us this Cultural Revolution garbage and pontificated to us about the merits of infanticide also want us to believe that guns are the real issue here. Unfortunately it is the depravity of people. Almost seven times more people were killed with knives last year than rifles of any kind and caliber. Twice as many people were killed with hands and feet.

Until we stop trying to make guns illegal and start trying to repair the forty plus years of moral decay and rot, my generation will always be known as the generation of Sex, Drugs and Lock n' Load.

ABOUT THE AUTHOR

Mark Mayberry lives in Tennessee and is pursuing a Law Degree. He hopes to work in politics and law after graduating. He is also a staff writer at TruthAboutBills.org and is the operator of GuerrillaPolitics.net. Mark is an avid outdoorsman and enjoys spending time hunting and fishing as well as with his family. You can reach Mark on Facebook and Twitter as well as his website GuerrillaPolitics.net.

This is all about seizing an opportunity to control the masses. This has been part of the progressive agenda for years. Gun confiscation has been part of the liberal play book for almost 400 years now. It happened to my ancestor and yours and they're at it again right now in the U.S. of A. Those in power know that they can't control armed citizens and I guarantee you our National Guard boys won't be willingly disarming their friends and family.

GUN CONTROL = PEOPLE CONTROL

Written by S.C. Sherman

11 January 2013

Gun control really means people control. It's also not a new idea. It's been around since people with guns set foot on North America. My ancestor, Philip Sherman, was a Puritan. He was part of the Massachusetts Bay Colony led by "The Governor" John Winthrop. Young Philip arrived in Boston in 1632, a bright-eyed youth from Dedham, England. He left all that he knew behind and embarked on a new life relatively free from the constraints of the English Crown and the persecution that went with it. (If interested, I wrote an entire book on it, available at www.scsherman.com titled *Leaving Southfields*.)

How exciting it must have been with the whole world literally before him. It's an inspiring story of the heritage that many of us share. It's a tale of the human heart searching for freedom. A freedom found only on the shores of what would become America. A freedom almost always claimed through the use of force and secured with weapons. Whether you were a poor white guy from Europe or an enslaved African, freedom in America has always come with armed citizens standing for what's right.

I am sure my young ancestor was surprised when on November 20, 1637 he was publicly listed as one of seventy-five individuals required to "…surrender to the appropriate authorities, all pistols, guns, swords, powder and matches, and any other weapon of warfare not listed, immediately. Furthermore, those listed are instructed to refrain from purchasing and or borrowing any weapons to replace those surrendered."

History repeats itself. Didn't a newspaper just publicly post the names of innocent gun owners? Yep, sure did.

Back in the Colonies, there was no "Sandy Hook" or "Columbine". No reason to control guns, right? Everyone hunted for food so everyone needed guns; there were no thirty-round magazines, no collapsible stocks, nothing mean-looking at all! There were definitely no guns called "Assault" weapons. There wasn't even a Second Amendment. They had single-shot black powder weapons and matches! Unless of course, you were lucky enough to have a newer 'flint-lock' model. If these colonials had none of the modern day reasons to disarm citizens, why did it happen back then too? You see, it's never really the guns that need controlling, it's the people. That's the dirty little secret.

My ancestor, Philip, had fallen in with a bad crowd. You know the kind of people who cling to their guns and Bibles. Anne Hutchinson was a judge's wife and quite popular with average folk. She was a midwife, loved babies, and pretty much knew the Bible front to back in her own right. She liked to gather friends in her home and talk about the spiritual topics of the day. It turns out that was a little more than those in power could stand. Meeting and talking about the Bible and a woman too. Didn't she know her place? Well the political elite showed her. They tossed her in jail with charges of sedition and heresy.

Wasn't there a guy in California that just got thrown in jail for having illegal home Bible meetings? Yep, sure was.

Anne Hutchinson was a good friend of my ancestor Philip and his wife Sarah, so when John Winthrop banished her to the wilds, they came for her friends as well. Philip's name was on the list to be disarmed. So what crime had Philip committed? None of course, just like all of us right now in the crosshairs of the Obama/Feinstein liberal mob. Philip didn't do anything and neither have we, other than hang out with the wrong sort of people and believe something contrary to those in power. Is it seditious to believe the 2nd Amendment literally means all citizens have the right to bear arms? Some think so.

People in power universally understand one thing. They can't allow the Average Joe's of the world to remain armed if they want to subdue them. The power players of the seventeenth century had no problem banishing a harmless forty-year-old woman, but the thought of seventy-five armed men presented a real problem. Governor Winthrop had a brilliant idea. Publicly name the trouble-makers, ridicule them, paint them as fringe, intimidate them, threaten them, blame them, turn their neighbors against them, and ultimately require them to bend a knee and voluntarily turn in their personal defense arms. How twenty-first century of them.

What can be done when the Government puts you on a list of folks to be disarmed and publicly names you? There are three choices; comply, fight, or flee. Philip and his crazy friends decided to set out on their own. They had had enough. Philip took his pregnant wife and their two children and fled to what became Rhode Island. Oh yeah, he took his guns with him. He later became the first Secretary of State of Rhode Island. It has to just chap those Rhode Island lefties today to know they were founded by a bunch of gun-loving radicals whose main goal in life was to worship their Christian Lord as they saw fit. Now they won't even call a Christmas tree by its name.

Be careful who your friends are. Apparently, that old adage has been true for centuries. So what is my crime? NRA life member is one problem. Then there's my carry permit, my Louis L'Amour collection, then of course writing for Clash Daily alone puts me in bad company and definitely on the list of citizens to watch. So when they come for Doug Giles, an outspoken gun-loving Bible-thumper, they will be coming for his friends too. That means me and maybe you. You see this has nothing to do with all of the innocent blood shed by psychos. That would be a mental health issue that we refuse to address.

This is all about seizing an opportunity to control the masses. This has been part of the progressive agenda for years. Gun confiscation has been part of the liberal play book for almost 400 years now. It happened to my ancestor and yours and they're at it again right now in the U.S. of A. Those in power know that they can't control armed citizens and I guarantee you our National Guard boys won't be willingly disarming their friends and family.

The rabid pacifists are growing in their chest-beating bravado. Failure to achieve their desires of a gun-free universe has raised their level of desperation and escalated them to a fever pitch. Recently a worn-out, old lefty from my neck of the woods, Donald Kaul, actually stated that the well known refrain, 'you can have my gun when you pry it from my cold dead hand' might be a fine way to handle us crazy gun-toters! Well that is easier said than done you whack-job-hippie! That's not just a catchy slogan to a lot of people. Blowing pot-smoke rings in our faces isn't going to make us drop our weapons and buy turtle-necks. I say "good luck" to your U.N. cops. I would take ten midwestern deer hunters against your European yahoos any day. Bring it on!

The recent tragedy in Newtown is a golden opportunity for the gun-grabbers to go for all they can get. But this is also our moment. We can't flee to Rhode Island, or anywhere really, it's time for gun-loving patriots to stand up and defend our freedoms. I for one am ready and willing to argue, write, and speak out wherever need be. No more quietly sitting by. Join me in the fray. Now is the time to stiffen your backbone and have firm resolve. Cold dead hands…I hope not, but this is worth dying for. Many others have already paid this price for the freedom we tenuously enjoy. They must disarm us to fully control us. Philip and his friends wouldn't accept being disarmed, we shouldn't either.

> *"Those who hammer their guns into plows will plow for those who do not."*
>
> *— Thomas Jefferson*

About the Author

S.C. Sherman grew up a farm kid in rural Iowa. He graduated from the University of Iowa with a degree in Communications Studies. Steve is a business owner, and recently ran for Iowa State House of Representatives.. S.C. enjoys political commentary and great stories. He has written three fiction novels found at www.scsherman.com He currently lives with his wife and four children in North Liberty, Iowa.

Do not be fooled by a belief that progressives, leftists hate guns ... they do not. What they hate is guns in the hands of those who are not marching in lock step of their ideology. They hate guns in the hands of those who think for themselves and do not obey without question.

Gun Control: Even Socialist Media Gets It

Written By Marilyn Assenheim

12 January 2013

Pravda, in Russian, means "truth". Don't get the wrong idea; I am definitely not a fan of Socialist cant, tiresomely palmed off as truth. But, as the saying goes, even a broken clock is correct twice a day. An article appeared in the English version of Pravda on December 28, 2012. It was written by Stanislav Mishin and is titled "*Americans Never Give up Your Guns*" . It is clear we have a genuine, national crisis on our hands when Pravda gets it right and the government, spearheaded by our president, gets it wrong.

Attempts to shred the Second Amendment are nothing new. There has been a determined effort to wrest guns from our nation's populace for half a century or better. The latest full-court press, which includes escalating statements from the president and the vice fool, promising to bypass Congress (again) "if necessary" to restrict gun ownership, is the latest liberal push to create a problem that has never existed. It doesn't matter how many facts contradict liberal talking points on gun ownership. The proof that a gun in the hands of responsible citizens deters crime does not seem to matter. Statistics proving that deaths caused by methods other than firearms (including murders committed using hammers) outnumber deaths caused by guns are, apparently, irrelevant. The desperation to eliminate gun ownership as a Constitutional right is under full sail.

There should be no need to reiterate what happens to a populace once disarmed by their government. There's more than enough historical evidence of the disastrous results when the only armed segment of the population is the ruling class. The current, lemming-like sprint to get rid of American's only protection against government incursion, however, makes Mr. Mishin's article all the more vital.

Mr. Mishin informs the reader that Russia used to be one of the most heavily armed nations on earth. This was, of course, when Russia was "free", under the Tsar. Mr. Mishin illuminates how citizens of countries that gave up gun ownership rights to their respective governments (such as Russia, Poland, France and Germany) suffered for their mistake. He debunks widespread, liberal dogma: "The excuse that people will start shooting each other is … silly. So it is our politicians saying that our society is full of incapable adolescents who can never be trusted? Then … explain how we can trust them or the police, who themselves grew up and came from the same culture?" One might further ask how it is that a public capable of electing temporary, government officials is deemed incapable of governing their own lives and welfare.

Mr. Mishin tells a serious, cautionary tale. His point is, you should pardon the expression, right on "target." Liberals are desperate for gun control solely for power: "Government will use the excuse of trying to protect the people from maniacs and crime …No, it is about power and a total power over the people. Do not be fooled by a belief that progressives, leftists hate guns … they do not. What they hate is guns in the hands of those who are not marching in lock step of their ideology. They hate guns in the hands of those who think for themselves and do not obey without question."

Pravda.

About the Author

Marilyn Assenheim was born and raised in New York City. She is a first generation American. Her parents were Holocaust survivors and LEGAL immigrants to this great country. She spent a career in healthcare management although she probably should have been a casting director or a cowboy. She is a serious devotee of history and politics, Marilyn currently lives in the NYC metropolitan area.

No, I think we should point our policy and derision not upon firearms but rather upon crappy parents who don't raise their kids right or who don't rein them in when they're going off the rails on a crazy train.

MASSACRE SOLUTION: THE BRADY BUNCH BILL TO PROHIBIT THE PROCREATION OF IRRESPONSIBLE PEOPLE

Written By Doug Giles

13 January 2013

As most of you know, vice president Joe Biden has been appointed by Obama to make certain that another Sandy Hook never goes down on American soil. Being an American who digs freedom, I'm not getting the warm and fuzzies about this legislative venture. A myopic cyclops staring into the sun can see where this duo is heading.

And as most of you can guess, Biden and Obama are talking about levying an executive order on our populace that would ban certain semi-automatic rifles and high capacity pistol and rifle magazines. It's a similar policy to the Clinton Assault Weapons Ban that did nada to stem school and workplace violence from 1994 to 2004. Matter of fact, school shootings spiked during that epoch. What is it they say about the definition of insanity?

Anyway, as the Left gears up to bear down on law-abiding people because some demoniac's murder spree has left us all reeling, I would like to put forth a proposal that doesn't mitigate our constitutional right to keep and bear arms but rather makes it more difficult for people to hook up and breed. It's an expanded version of what Dennis Miller alluded to back in the mid '90s—namely the Brady Bunch Bill: a waiting period before people get married and start a family.

Yes, I'm more worried about high capacity idiots than I am about high capacity magazines. Look, you and I can ban such tools all day long, but demented tools will still find a way to get at them or switch deadly devices. For some reason evil people won't obey our laws. Indeed, the crazy will search for other ways to McVeigh us into McSmithereens. BTW, all Timothy needed was fertilizer and a Ryder truck; an extended magazine didn't come close to accomplishing what that satanic soul had in mind. Should we ban ammonium nitrate, nitromethane, racing fuel and rental trucks?

No, I think we should point our policy and derision not upon firearms but rather upon crappy parents who don't raise their kids right or who don't rein them in when they're going off the rails on a crazy train. Pardon me for sounding simplistic, but until people who wish to bump uglies and have kids prove to us that they're going to superintend their brood into becoming an amicable part of the American collective, I say we prohibit their reproductive rights.

Check it out. Here's what I propose: Those desirous to mate or adopt would have to pass a thorough psychological and criminal background check and a five-year (at least) proving period where they would have to affirm the following:

1. Will you stay married and work your crap out so that it doesn't decimate your children to the degree that they one day take their rage out on kindergartners?

2. Will you raise your kids to obey the Golden Rule? No? Well then … forced sterilization for you.

3. Will you love and nurture your offspring versus pawning their upbringing off on satanic pop culture, violent videos, paranormal peers and Hollywood death flicks? Huh, D-bag?

4. Will you refuse to allow your kid to have a petty entitlement mentality and a woe-is-me vengeful spirit of hatred?

5. Will you quit going about business as usual if your kid starts worshipping Satan and giggles when he hears or sees people murdered or raped?

6. Will you turn your kid in if he begins talking to imaginary people while stockpiling a weapons cache that rivals a small nation's battery?

7. Will you, in the event that the aforementioned has not helped to move your kid away from the morose, refuse to teach your child how to shoot and either get rid of your weapons or lock them in a vault that he cannot crack nor move with a Hyster 36-48T forklift?

8. And finally, will you take full responsibility (to the point of prosecution and imprisonment) if your teen or twentysomething kid kills

anyone because you have fundamentally failed doing your duties as a parent?

If a couple cannot answer in the affirmative and do not show responsible and respectful behavior during the preliminary five-year waiting period then we disallow said couple to breed. How's that?

Look, folks, we can ban all manner of weapons until the cows come home, but until parents start raising their kids right and steer them clear of this rancid culture this junk is going to plague us 'til the end of time.

Finally, my advice to the policy wonks is this: Until the Brady Bunch Bill is put into effect, stay the hell away from our guns because we're going to need the wherewithal to put down your bad seed should he attempt to kill our innocent sons and daughters.

About Doug Giles

Doug Giles is the man behind ClashDaily.com. In addition to driving ClashDaily.com, Giles is a popular columnist on Townhall.com and the author of the book Raising Righteous & Rowdy Girls.

Doug's articles have also appeared on several other print and online news sources, including The Washington Times, The Daily Caller, Fox Nation, USA Today, The Wall Street Journal, The Washington Examiner, The Blaze, American Hunter Magazine and ABC News.

He's been a frequent guest on the Fox News Channel and Fox Business Channel as well as many nationally syndicated radio shows across the nation — which, he believes, officially makes him a super hero.

In addition, Doug is an occasional guest host on New York City's WABC (The Jason Mattera Show) and he is a weekly guest, every Friday at 7:45am[et], on America's Morning News (155 markets).

Giles and his wife Margaret have two daughters: Hannah, who devastated ACORN with her 2009 nation shaking undercover videos, and Regis who is an NRA columnist, huntress and Second Amendment activist.

DG's interests include guns, big game hunting, big game fishing, fine art, cigars, helping wounded warriors, and being a big pain in the butt to people who dislike God and the USA.

Read more Doug Giles at www.clashdaily.com.

As someone who has actively embraced the tenets of the Christian faith, my beliefs are in no way offended by the heart-felt petitions offered up by someone of another faith.

A 'Ten Commandments' Solution to Our School Problems

Written By R.G. Yoho

14 January 2013

Many of you reading this column can look back with fondness over your school years.

Some of you may have gone to one-room schoolhouses. Others among you attended a more conventional school, much like mine. But no matter what kind of school you attended, I doubt that many of you experienced the kinds of violence you are constantly reading about in your daily newspapers.

Was that simply a fluke? Or has something else changed?

Although God had already been expelled from some of the bigger city schools, I attended a rural elementary school that started each day with prayer and the Pledge of Allegiance. I can even remember seeing the "Ten Commandments" posted on the blackboards in some of the classrooms.

To make matters worse, nearly every guy in our high school carried a pocket knife, something that would now be considered a dangerous weapon. The boys routinely used to brag about whose blade had the sharpest edge, something that often led to heated discussions among them.

In addition, it wasn't unusual for the boys in my high school to have shotguns in their vehicles, especially if they were going hunting or shooting after the final bell rang for the day.

However, despite the fact that many of us were armed with knives or firearms at school, those items were never used to settle disputes between the students.

That's why the Good Lord gave us fists.

Yet despite all of these unsavory influences in my elementary and secondary education, I somehow managed not to wander into a life of crime and debauchery.

Apparently, nobody has ever been irreparably harmed by godly influences in their early education.

But now that God has been forcibly expelled from our schools, perhaps someone needs to ask America how that approach is working out for them.

If our children were once again openly exposed to the Ten Commandments at school, they would come under such dangerous concepts such as "Thou shalt not steal" and "Thou shalt not kill."

And God forbid! What would happen if the children started to believe and practice these ideas? What could be the worst thing that might happen?

Perhaps they might not cheat off their friends' papers or shoot their fellow students and teachers.

If they actually saw the words, "Neither shalt thou covet," perhaps these students wouldn't grow up to join the Occupy Movement, thinking they routinely deserved to pick the fruits of another man's labors.

And what if they learned those outdated notions about not bearing false witness or having their neighbor's wife? Shoot! Those two commandments would no doubt eliminate most of our representatives in Congress.

As someone who has actively embraced the tenets of the Christian faith, my beliefs are in no way offended by the heart-felt petitions offered up by someone of another faith.

Moreover, I am a Christian who has never felt threatened by the prayers of a Jewish rabbi.

The Ten Commandments are prominently posted on the wall where the Supreme Court meets. Congress begins their daily sessions with a word of prayer. And we stamp the words, "In God We Trust" on our money.

If faith is good enough for our judges and elected officials, then why isn't it good enough for our children in public and private schools?

If acknowledgements of God and moments of prayer can receive a place in our public schools after a tragedy occurs, then maybe it's time we should consider inviting God back into our schools before the next one occurs.

ABOUT THE AUTHOR

Author R.G. Yoho is the author of three Westerns, including "Death Comes to Redhawk."

In addition to his Westerns, R.G. recently published a work of non-fiction, "America's History is His Story."

Please check out his Author's Page on Facebook: http://www.Facebook.com/R.G.Yoho

But Obama must think he is the honey badger. One thing is certain, and that is he doesn't care. He takes what he wants, whether it be people's guns, money, property, or their rights.

Obama's Executive Orders in Defiance of the Constitution

Written By Andrew Linn

14 January 2013

In the midst of the gun control debate, as well as the arguments over the national debt, there is the chance Obama might bypass Congress and instead rely on Executive Orders to push forth his agenda.

Joe Biden is recommending that Obama issue gun control regulations via Executive Order. Biden met with pro-gun and anti-gun groups in the past few days in an attempt to work out a solution. While meeting with the pro-gun groups, I wonder if he tried to rely on the same bizarre behavior he used in the Vice Presidential debate with Paul Ryan.

Meanwhile, Harry Reid is recommending the same tactic for the debt ceiling.

Such suggestions demonstrate the Obama Administration's (and its supporters) disregard for the Constitution.

An Executive Order is an order by the President given to departments and agencies within the Executive Department to carry out laws or policies passed by Congress. However, some Executive Orders have been contrary to Congressional intentions, or the Constitution for that matter. One example would be Clinton issuing Executive Order 12852 in 1993, establishing a Council of Sustainable Development in order to advance Agenda 21.

Now Obama wishes to implement his policies via Executive Order, since gun control legislation is unlikely to pass in Congress, and since there has been practically a standstill over the national debt.

But Obama must think he is the honey badger. One thing is certain, and that is he doesn't care. He takes what he wants, whether it be people's guns, money, property, or their rights.

And neither do his supporters. Harry Belafonte wanted him to act like a Third World dictator and put Republicans in jail. Woody Allen wanted Obama to be a dictator in order to get things done.

Apparently Biden and Reid feel the same way.

And to make matters worse, there is a bill in Congress to repeal the Twenty-Second Amendment, thus eliminating presidential term limits. Obama would no doubt love that idea, since it would give him a chance to be in the White House indefinitely (if not for life).

I guess since Obama was re-elected, some liberals think conservatives will just cave in to his agenda. But they are quite mistaken. The American people will not surrender their rights guaranteed to them in the Constitution, and that includes the Second Amendment. Americans will not surrender their freedom to Obama, nor to the United Nations.

ABOUT THE AUTHOR

Andrew Linn is a member of the Owensboro Tea Party and a former Field Representative for the Media Research Center. An ex-Democrat, he became a Republican one week after the 2008 Presidential Election. He has an M.A. in history from the University of Louisville, where he became a member of the Phi Alpha Theta historical honors society. He has also contributed to examiner.com and Right Impulse Media.

Our Founders thought there would be many revolutions in our history. They thought blood would have to be spilt every few decades to ensure that we remain committed to the freedom of the individual.

HAS THE SECOND AMENDMENT FAILED?

Written By Irwin Podhajser

14 January 2013

There has been a lot of debate lately about gun control. After the Connecticut school shooting I wrote my opinions.

I am a proud owner of a 1911 Colt .45 and enjoy my right to bear arms; and unlike most Americans I understand the amendment that gives me that right. I didn't weigh in on the gun control issue at that time, but now I believe it is time to do so. The problem with debating gun control is that most people on both sides simply don't seem to understand the Second Amendment. That's where we will start and end our conversation today. Since it is a complicated and emotional issue, there are several points I want to make here.

The Second Amendment Does Not Limit Any Arms Ownership – There are those that argue that there are limits on your Second Amendment rights just like there are limits on the First Amendment and the protection of free speech, such as you don't have the right to yell "Fire" in a crowded theater or you don't have the right to libel someone.

These arguments are wrong. In the early days of the Republic, the average citizens could arm themselves with the same weapon that the army had. Bring that into the modern era and not only do people have the right to automatic weapons; you could argue they have the rights to own tanks and fighter planes.

The other bad comparison is that the limits on free speech are only enacted when your freedom interferes with the freedom of another individual. You have freedom of speech, you just can't use it to limit the freedom of others, just like you have the rights to bear any arms you like as long as you don't limit the freedom of others with that right.

There Is A Proper Way To Change The Second Amendment – My problem with gun control advocates is not their arguments for gun control, but the way they go about trying to achieve it. If you want to limit our right to bear arms, then do it the way the Constitution says to do it; through a constitutional amendment. Let's have this debate state by state and let the people decide whether they want to give up their right to bear arms. Let's have the debate and really educate America on why we have the Second Amendment. If we repeal or amend the Second Amendment through the right means, I can live with that. I might not like it, but I can live with it.

The Right To Bear Arms Only Works In A Moral Society – As I said in my original article, the problem in the school shootings is evil, not the right to bear arms. The problem we are facing in this country is that we are becoming a more immoral and evil people. Evil has always been with us and it always will be with us, but our society is simply degenerating which allows this evil to flourish in the open rather than hiding in dark corners. We are paying the price for the lack of boundaries and the concept of "do what makes you feel good". We are paying the price for a society that, in the name of "tolerance", has blurred the line between right and wrong and has declared God dead. Forget the war on guns, let's have a war on immorality.

The Second Amendment Has Failed – You can ignore every point above, because it all comes down to this final observation that the Second Amendment has failed. We have missed the whole point behind why the amendment exists in the first place. The reason behind the amendment and the entire Bill of Rights is to endow the individual with so much freedom and so much power that it would keep the government in check. The philosophy was that the "people should not fear their government; the government should fear their people". The Second Amendment was there to arm the people so that the government could never take any of the other freedoms away.

The only problem is that what the government couldn't take by force, they have gotten through trickery. We have slowly given away our freedoms and have empowered the one institution our founders feared the most. Out of fear and laziness we have traded liberty for protection. We have traded freedom for a giant nanny.

There is a scene in *Star Wars Episode 3* where two senators are watching a speech by the high chancellor. In the speech, the chancellor, in the name of safe and secure society, restructures the republic into an empire and proclaims himself the emperor. The crowd rises in applause. One of the two senators says to the other, "So this is how liberty dies. By thunderous applause."

Think about it. Our founders started a war over a tea tax. Now we have protests demanding higher taxes. We elect people who promise to tax us and to take care of us by robbing us of our freedoms and choices. Our Founders thought there would be many revolutions in our history. They thought blood would have to be spilt every few decades to ensure that we remain committed to the freedom of the individual. They knew of the danger of a too powerful government. What they didn't foresee was that, given enough time, the individual would rather choose a false sense of security over true freedom.

One program at a time. One freedom at a time. One by one we have handed it to a government that's only concern is power and it has all happened to the sound of thunderous applause. This is how amendments and liberty die.

About the Author

Irwin has had an eclectic line of careers including 15 years as a Miami youth pastor, media buyer and television executive. He is currently the President of DrTV Network which is a multi-level television network dedicated towards healthy living. He also serves as Chairman for The Advanced Television Broadcasting Alliance.

I would be embarrassed to show anyone this video as a defense for the Second Amendment, or watch it in public lest someone begins to wonder if I am clinically insane. While Jones makes some really good points, they are all muddled by his belligerent delivery.

DEFENDING OUR GUN RIGHTS?
CHILL OUT, ALEX JONES

Written By Andres Ortiz

14 January 2013

After watching the Piers Morgan CNN interview with Alex Jones this week I was sorely disappointed in the way our pro-Second Amendment message was portrayed by our libertarian brother. I do not mean that we should have someone with the fluffiness of Joel Osteen as an advocate for our gun rights, as I rather enjoyed watching Ted Nugent and Jesse Ventura put Morgan in his place on the guns topic. I always prefer a hearty discussion on controversial topics, in fact I seek it out. After all, I am a huge Coulter fan.

This interview, however, was more resembling of Uncle Ted after ten shots of Jameson and a pound of beef jerky at a bar fight. Jones was not letting Morgan get a word or question in edgewise and when he did, he would vaguely answer the question and then go off on a rant about "Suicide pills! Mass murder pills!"

Maybe I am alone in this with my Clash Daily following but I would be embarrassed to show anyone this video as a defense for the Second Amendment, or watch it in public lest someone begins to wonder if I am clinically insane. While Jones makes some really good points, they are all muddled by his belligerent delivery. At one point, he even challenges Piers Morgan to a boxing match! Because there is no better time to challenge your national television host to a fight than when our country is debating whether people are sane enough to have guns.

Of course, Morgan was having a field day with Jones as he closed the interview by asking who he thought was responsible for bringing down the twin towers. During Alex's conspiracy rant, CNN had on the bottom of the screen

"Jones' Conspiracy Theories." Oh, and don't forget how Alex spent about a minute mocking Morgan's British accent. Are we back in middle school, guy?

Let's get this straight, Alex Jones is brought to CNN to talk about "Guns In America" as the segment was beautifully titled and it ends with him accusing "criminal elements of the military industrial complex" for 9/11 and past terrors on America. This is a reverse example of what Ann Coulter has said about liberals before: Liberals don't shun their crazies, they promote them and put them on the forefront. Now we have Jones on CNN trying to make our case by getting in his interviewer's face and ranting about a plethora of controversial subjects? No thank you.

We have to remember that our conservative message is grounded on the principles of Christianity and not the other way around. This doesn't mean that we have to be nicer than Christ; anyone that follows my past articles knows I have a huge disdain for the squishiness and timidity of the current American church. There is definitely a time and place for righteous indignation, to gird up your loins and fight for what you believe in.

But trying to outcrazy your opponent is not doing the rest of us a favor. So chill out, Alex Jones, gather your composure and go back on the show with just a handful of those great talking points you had and slam Morgan with your wisdom, not your voice or fists.

About the Author

Andres Ortiz is the video producer for ClashDaily.com, he is also a musician and much involved in the Christian underground scene filming concerts, interviews, and short documentaries for international touring acts. He has been a devoted member of Clash Church since late 2006. His projects include: Polycarp Media, The Saving, and Clash Worship.

Many in the anti-gun movement interpret "Militia" to mean the military or national guard. EAAAAAAAHHHH!!! (Buzzer sound) I'm sorry, that answer is incorrect.

SECOND AMENDMENT DEBATE: RIGHTS VS. CREEPING T

Written By Audrey Russo

15 January 2013

"I ask, Sir, what is the militia? It is the whole people. To disarm the people is the best and most effectual way to enslave them." —George Mason, Co-author of the Second Amendment during Virginia's Convention to Ratify the Constitution, 1788

Our Founders were perspicacious men. What they established 237 years ago has brought peace and freedom to millions, to the chagrin of Tyrants, Ruling Class wannabes and their ilk of every stripe.

These prescient designers based the founding of the world's greatest experiment upon immutable principles...not amorphous ideas that change with the shifting winds of man's whimsy. These precepts, based upon inalienable rights, set the solid, unshakable foundation that has served our republic well for more than two centuries. This is not to say that these principles have not been challenged... they have...and have stood the test of time and nimrods, since our inception.

The difference between those challenges and today's is the people. Today they bully their way to grab the narrative...and pretend to use facts, but rather use half truths or lies cloaked as truth, in order to reason with the citizenry.

Clearly, if you've ever encountered those on the wrong side of this debate (and the wrong side is that which is against the Constitution), you'll find that not everyone in the anti-gun movement realizes that creeping tyranny (Creeping T) is the impetus behind their view...but it is indeed the big money Marxists, like Soros and his ilk, that are masquerading as the civilized, concerned community.

Those of us who love our Constitution, would be glad to debate opponents of the Second Amendment. But there's a problem: We come to the contest ready to lay out our arguments, with empirical evidence. They, on the other hand, are unable to come with integrity...because they refuse to reveal their true agenda: To ban all guns. Period. So they often bring intimidation via slander to the table.

And, as Socrates once said, *"When the debate is lost, slander is the tool of the loser."*

I'm simply going to deal with the most misused and abused clause, by those afflicted by Hoplophobia (the morbid, irrational fear of guns): Militia.

Here is the Second Amendment of our Bill of Rights:

"A well regulated Militia being necessary to the security of a free State, the right of the people to keep and bear Arms shall not be infringed."

But it was NOT left to interpretation by those who live in a Silly Putty nebulous world.

Many in the anti-gun movement interpret "Militia" to mean the military or national guard. EAAAAAAAHHHH!!! (Buzzer sound) I'm sorry, that answer is incorrect.

According to the Federalist Papers, written by John Jay, James Madison and Alexander Hamilton...what the Founding Fathers (authors of the Second Amendment) considered a "Militia" to be was "All able bodied men" not a government power or agency.

Not good enough answer for the 'only Cops and the Military should have guns' crowd?

Okee Dokee...how about another brainiac by the name of St. George Tucker, a lawyer, Revolutionary War militia officer, legal scholar, and later a U.S. District Court judge (appointed by James Madison in 1813), who wrote of the Second Amendment in his popular edition of Blackstone's Commentaries of the Laws of England (with Notes of Reference to the The Constitution and Laws of the Federal Government of the United States and of the Commonwealth of Virginia [1803]):

"The right of the people to keep and bear arms shall not be infringed, and this without any qualification as to their condition or degree, as is the case in the British government."

And in the Appendix:

"This may be considered as the true palladium of liberty... The right of self-defense is the first law of nature; in most governments it has been the study of rulers to confine this right within the narrowest limits possible. Whenever standing armies are kept up, and the right of the people to keep and bear arms is, under any color or pretext whatsoever, prohibited, liberty, if not already annihilated, is on the brink of destruction. In England, the people have been disarmed, generally, under the specious pretext of preserving the game: a never failing lure to bring over the landed aristocracy to support any measure, under that mask, though calculated for very different purposes. True it is, their bill of rights seems at first view to counteract this policy: but the right of bearing arms is confined to Protestants, and the words suitable to their condition and degree, have been interpreted to authorise the prohibition of keeping a gun or other engine for the destruction of game, to any farmer, or inferior tradesman, or other person not qualified to kill game. So that not one man in five hundred can keep a gun in his house without being subject to a penalty."

(Did you catch the part the earth-embracers should love: "The right of self-defense is the first law of nature." That's pretty organic.)

Tucker's evidence is unequivocal: The ' militia' clause was NOT intended to restrict the right to keep arms to active militia members, but he speaks of a broader right: The right to self-defense.

The facts, ad nauseum (but apparently not enough to penetrate the heads of Hoplophobics), have been presented by far greater people than I...but the point is clear for those who are mentally capable of comprehension:

Concerning the Second Amendment, the Founders and I agree: This is MY right to stop Creeping T.

God Bless the US Constitution!

ABOUT THE AUTHOR

Audrey Russo is the Host of the weekly REELTalk Radio Show and the co-host of WOMANTalk Radio Show. She handles Middle East Issues/National Security/Terrorism for their eZine and writes on foreign affairs for The Examiner.com. She guests on several radio shows including The Rick Amato Show, The Simon Conway Show, The Pat Campbell Show and The Mike Wiley Show. Audrey is the Managing Editor for the online opinion journal Ediblog.com. Her articles can also be read at The Center for Changing Worldviews and the Gold Coast Chronicle as well as other online journals. She is also an active member of the NYC performing arts community as a singer and actor.

Logic would dictate that the Bill of Rights applied equally to the Federal government and the States. After all, why would we protect certain rights, then give states the ability to infringe on them?

SCOTUS AND GUN CONTROL, PART 2

Written by Suzanne Olden

15 January 2013

I last discussed the 2008 Supreme Court of the United States ("SCOTUS") decision District of Columbia v. Heller in which the Court held that banning handguns or making citizens keep them unusable is unconstitutional. Today we are going to look at the 2010 SCOTUS decision McDonald v. City of Chicago, III., 130 S. Ct. 3020 (2010). Same issue, with a twist.

This case also dealt with a handgun ban. The City of Chicago had an ordinance that stated: "[n]o person shall... possess ... any firearm unless such person is the holder of a valid registration certificate for such firearm." It then went on to prohibit registration of most handguns, thus effectively banning handgun possession. The Village of Oak Park also had a law that made it 'unlawful for any person to possess ... any firearm," and then made the term "firearm" include "pistols, revolvers, guns and small arms ... commonly known as handguns." After the Heller decision in 2008, several residents of both locations sued to enforce their Second Amendment rights.

Our laws are built on the idea of precedent of stare decises. Stare decises is Latin for "to stand by things decided." It means, generally, that courts will adhere to the previous ruling to make a new ruling. Chicago and Oak Lawn argue that their laws are constitutional because the Second Amendment doesn't apply to the States. SCOTUS had previously held that most of the provisions of the Bill of Rights apply with full force to both the Federal Government and the States. Precedent said that the Second Amendment right is and should be applied fully to the States.

Interestingly enough, SCOTUS acknowledged in its decision that Chicago Police Department statistics reveal that the City's handgun murder rate has actually increased since the ban was enacted. The City has one of the highest murder and violent crime rates in the US. The ban did NOT make Chicago safer, as proponents stated it would.

The residents who sued argued that the ban violated their Second Amendment rights for two reasons. First reason was that the Second Amendment falls among those rights called the The Privileges or Immunities Clause. Second, the residents argued that the Due Process Clause of the Fourteenth Amendment incorporates the Second Amendment. History on this is interesting, and it evolved… a lot.

Logic would dictate that the Bill of Rights applied equally to the Federal government and the States. After all, why would we protect certain rights, then give states the ability to infringe on them? However, that wasn't the original intent. The Bill of Rights, including the Second Amendment, originally applied only to the Federal Government, and in the 19th century it became a huge enough issue that we fought a Civil War over it. After the Civil War, the Fourteenth Amendment was adopted. It states "All persons born or naturalized in the United States, and subject to the jurisdiction thereof, are citizens of the United States and of the state wherein they reside. No state shall make or enforce any law which shall abridge the privileges or immunities of citizens of the United States; nor shall any state deprive any person of life, liberty, or property, without due process of law; nor deny to any person within its jurisdiction the equal protection of the laws." Clear enough, right? Well, not so fast. It took decades to get to the place where we are today.

Also, The Privileges or Immunities Clause was narrowly defined as to not include the Bill of Rights in an early case decided by SCOTUS called the Slaughter-House Cases. That changed as well. "Privileges or immunities" were a fancy way of saying rights. Interestingly enough, this narrow definition didn't change until the current case was decided.

Initially after the adoption of the Fourteenth Amendment, the Court initially found that rights that predated the Constitution weren't protected by it. In other words, they skirted the Fourteenth Amendment. Slowly the Court began a process that was called "selective incorporation" under the Due Process Clause. Rights like the First Amendment right to peaceably assemble were found to be a "fundamental right… safeguarded by the due process clause of the Fourteenth Amendment." Eventually, the Court began to speak of rights that are "so rooted in the traditions and conscience of our people as to be ranked as fundamental." Eventually the Court held that due process prohibits a State from taking private property without just compensation (eminent domain) and that people can't be compelled to incriminate themselves on a State level, instead of just a Federal one. One by one, the rights protected in the Bill of Rights were selectively incorporated by the Fourteenth Amendment. Finally, in the 1950's the Court abandoned the idea that the Fourteenth Amendment could be "watered down" in its application to the States. SCOTUS decisively held that the Bill of Rights protections "are all to be enforced against the States under the Fourteenth Amendment according to the same standards that protect those personal rights against federal encroachment."

This lead to the holding, or decision, in McDonald. The Court stated "In Heller, we held that the Second Amendment protects the right to possess a handgun in the home for the purpose of self-defense. Unless considerations of stare decisis counsel otherwise, a provision of the Bill of Rights that protects a right that is fundamental from an American perspective applies equally to the Federal Government and the States... We therefore hold that the Due Process Clause of the Fourteenth Amendment incorporates the Second Amendment right recognized in Heller." With that, the case was sent back to the state courts for further action in keeping with this decision.

These are two important decisions. They tell us as citizens that our State and Federal governments cannot take away our Second Amendment rights by selectively banning weapons, by refusing to allow the registration of weapons effectively banning all weapons, or by making citizens keep weapons in a manner that makes them inoperable. We have rights, and Obama and his gun commission should keep in mind that precedent is on our side, not theirs.

ABOUT THE AUTHOR

Suzanne Reisig Olden is a Catholic Christian, Conservative, married mother of two. She lives northwest of Baltimore, in Carroll County, Maryland. She graduated of Villa Julie College/Stevenson University with a BS in Paralegal Studies and works as a paralegal for a franchise company, specializing in franchise law and intellectual property. Originally from Baltimore, and after many moves, she came home to raise her son and daughter, now ages 17 and 13, in her home state. Suzanne also writes for the online publication, *The Beacon Bulletin*.

Read more of her work at http://beaconbulletin.com/.

The article, apparently requiring the skills of three writers, was clearly meant to incite anger, rage, annoyance, and a bunch of other verbs at the NRA.

NRA App — Important "News"?

Written By Pauline Wolak

16 January 2013

It's interesting what the *New York Daily News* considers "news." Current Editor's Picks include Olivia Wilde's engagement ring and Kim Kardashian's due date. I'm sure I'll sleep more soundly tonight knowing Brittany Spears was able to "step out" after her breakup with whatever it was that was stupid enough to date her.

With important headlines like that, it's not surprising that they actually printed the following story, *"NRA spits on the graves of Newtown massacre victims with release of mobile shoot-'em-up app for iPhone, iPad."*

Given the headline, I was sure this was going to be insightful, well-reasoned, and accurate. (I can't even type that with a straight face). The article, apparently requiring the skills of three writers, was clearly meant to incite anger, rage, annoyance, and a bunch of other verbs at the NRA. I do appreciate the way they subtly threw in the "sign our online petition to ban assault weapons" link. (By subtle, I mean 14 pt, caps locked, and in bright blue font).

The app in question, called *NRA: Practice Range* is pretty much what the title implies. For anyone that's ever been to a range, it's pretty familiar stuff. You pick a weapon. You shoot at targets. What the article coined as "coffin-shaped," the rest of us know as silhouette targets. True to the article, you CAN choose your weapon. You DO shoot at things. A four year old COULD access this app.

Here's what the article left out or barely touched on. The main menu offers a link entitled, *"NRA Info."* Clicking the link allows you to learn more about things like gun safety, guns laws, legislation, hunting season and NRA news. If you click on the individual games, you get a "fact." For instance, fact #3 states,

"Over the last 50 years, the NRA has trained more than 50,000 law enforcement firearm instructors and currently have over 11,000 instructors."

I daresay, even the good folks at *NY Daily News* appreciate our well-armed and well-trained police officers.

The app's rating is merely that, a rating. Cooking Light is rated 4+ as well. Do you think my four year old is going to use that? I shouldn't have to mention this, but I would like to point out that most four year olds don't own or control their own iPad, iPod, or iPhone. And if they do, they have bigger issues than an NRA app. The words "bad parents" come to mind here.

The Second Amendment protects our right to own guns, for hunting, for target shooting, or for display. As long as the reason is a legal one, why does the *NY Daily News* care? I'd think that any newspaper or entity would be happy that the NRA offers training courses, gun safety, etc. Instead they mock the following in their article, "always keep the gun pointed in a safe direction," "stop shooting immediately if you think you have experienced a gun malfunction" and "use only the correct ammunition for your gun." Why?

It seems to me their mock outrage would be better aimed at the person that developed the game *"Bullet to the Head of the NRA."* That's a game that actually promotes violence and murder. I guess it's more morally outrageous to shoot at a paper target than people who disagree with you politically.

ABOUT THE AUTHOR

Pauline is a proud stay-at-home wife and mother of three. By "at home" she means everywhere but home. She spends her time volunteering for various projects and charities as well as being "that mom" on the PTO and school board. After her family, she lives for coffee, football, and sharing her opinion with anyone that will (and sometimes won't) listen! She's an unabashed pro-life Catholic. Please follow her on Twitter at https://twitter.com/MiStateFan or visit clashdaily.com.

The real question that is behind the Second Amendment and the "alter and abolish" clause in the declaration is, "what does it take for thousands of sane people to pull the trigger?" The answer is tyranny!

AN ASSAULT WEAPON BY ANY OTHER NAME

Written By John Kirkwood

16 January 2013

Alright, I'll play along. Yes, I own an assault rifle and it is my right to own the assault rifle, the assault pistol, the assault slingshot, the assault knife and my most prized possession – the assault keyboard. The Second Amendment recognizes my God-given right to my assault rifle as the First Amendment recognizes my right to my assault tongue, my assault pen and my assault religion. You should be scared of them, Mr. President. Every would-be tyrant should fear a citizen who is armed with the knowledge, the weapons and the capacity of a free man.

So maybe I'm tired of the semantics. Call me the Eazy E of the gun debate but I embrace the moniker "assault weapon" as Eazy, Dre and Ice-cube embraced the N-word in N.W.A.; as my forefathers in Antioch embraced the Roman slur "Christian." There are those who would run from the term "assault weapon" because they know that leftist demagogues use the term to frighten low-information soccer moms. I don't run from it; I embrace it. I won't pretend that I need a ten-round magazine to shoot a deer or even to protect my crib. I need it to shoot the bastard or the tyrant who would have me in chains or try to take my guns.

Every weapon is an assault weapon. A #2 yellow Ticonderoga driven through an eye socket is an assault pencil. Now, I know that there will be those out there that cry out that their gun is for defense and that they'd only use it if they themselves are "assaulted"; and while I agree with this, I'm getting tired of hearing it. I don't need to apologize for my fundamental right to protect life and liberty, nor will I assume the defensive position merely because it's more politic.

You can trace this attitude of ritual emasculation back to the time that America traded the moniker "Department of War" for "Department of Defense." Tell me, did the boys of Pont du Hoc "assault" the beaches at Normandy or were they defending uphill? Did William Wallace take his sword and "assault" the English bastards trying to force submission or not? Did our fathers not raise righteous and menacing arms against the British with the intent to assault their limey backsides? Child, Please! Stow the euphemisms; I'm a free man.

In my lifetime, I have seen the left grow more brazen with their wish to disarm the American people. So bold are they that mayors, senators and presidents openly share their plans to "infringe" on our rights by fiat, while complicit journalists post the names and addresses of gun owners and an attorney general wishes to "brainwash" the American people against guns until they feel the "shame" that the cigarette smoker feels. The crust of an administration that has peddled "assault weapons" to Mexican drug cartels and Arab insurgencies and then dares tell honest, patriotic citizens that they must surrender their first and last lines of defense is beyond absurd.

"Let me be clear", Mr. President, not you nor Mayor's Bloomberg or Emanuel or Senator Feinstein or any group of men or women within this country or without, have the right to infringe on our freedom to keep and bear arms. The Second Amendment is non-negotiable. Your executive orders are just further evidence of your Imperial Presidency. They will be bad policy and bad precedent. George III didn't even have the brass to go about it in the manner that you have promoted.

The American people are putting you on notice that we will not be trifled with. You may raise our taxes but just try and take our guns. In the past two months, freedom loving Americans have purchased enough firearms to arm the entire Chinese Army and trust me, they're not buying them because they've been inspired by DUCK DYNASTY. These new gun owners are not hunters. They are buying guns because of you, Mr. President, because of your administration and the lapdog press that straightens your path and carries your water. They are buying guns because they know history and don't want their children to be future victims of the despotism that your jargon and propaganda presage.

Americans are buying guns at a rate this nation has never seen before because we rightly fear an Imperial Presidency and we know that we can't rely on an opposition party that doesn't have the intestinal fortitude to stand up to the statists on the other side of the aisle. There may be only a handful of statesmen in Washington that understand this moment, maybe only dozens of judges in the judiciary but let the gun sales around the country, let the shelves, empty of ammo, be a stern reminder to you that Americans prize their freedom more than they do mere mammon. Despots may feel that "from my cold dead hands" is an empty slogan from a bygone era but when it comes to disarming America, there will be, as Jefferson said, "the blood of patriots and tyrants" to refresh the tree of liberty.

The President and his complicit statist posse, have focused the attention on a crazy kid's access to guns, as if the Second Amendment can be blunted on the basis of what it took for one insane kid to pull the trigger. The real question that is behind the Second Amendment and the "alter and abolish" clause in the declaration is, "what does it take for thousands of sane people to pull the trigger?" The answer is tyranny! To those of you that desire to strip us of the tools of liberty, who would take our guns? Molon Labe! We'll be waiting and we'll leave the light on for you!

ABOUT THE AUTHOR

John Kirkwood is a son of Issachar. He is a Zionist, gun-toting, cigar-smoking, incandescent light bulb-using, 3.2 gallon flushing, fur-wearing, Chinese (MSG) eating, bow-hunting, SUV driving, unhyphenated American man who loves his wife, isn't ashamed of his country and does not apologize for his Christianity. He Pastors Grace Gospel Fellowship Bensenville, where "we the people" seek to honor "In God we Trust." He hosts the Christian wake up call IN THE ARENA every Sunday at noon on AM 1160 and he co-hosts Un-Common Sense, the Christian Worldview with a double shot of espresso on UncommonShow.com. He is the proud homeschooling dad of Konnor, Karter and Payton and the "blessed from heaven above" husband of the Righteous and Rowdy Wendymae.

The anti-gunners are in a tizzy right now, because the NRA just got 250,000 new members on the heels of a school shooting; and because guns are flying off shelves; and because the ammo store cupboards are bare. They're scratching their heads saying, "What the hell just happened?"

PRESIDENT OBAMA
A GUN OWNER'S BEST FRIEND

Written By Skip Coryell

17 January 2013

The other day I got a call from an old friend from college. I'd heard from him only a few times in the past thirty years, so I was a bit surprised. I was taken aback by his short and to the point email. It simply said: "Hi Skip, what is the best gun for self-defense?"

I had to think about that, because I had no idea why he was asking. I told him there was no single "best gun" for self defense, and then I took him and his ten-year-old son to the gun range. I didn't ask him point blank why this sudden interest in guns at age fifty-something. He was a city dweller, successful business executive, husband and father of two.

When we got to the range it was fifty-five degrees and sunny. Not bad for a January in Michigan. It's almost like God wanted us to be there. At least that's the way I took it. I took him through all the basics of safety and shooting, and then we threw some lead downrange. He was pretty good for a banker. And then his son wanted to try. I started him out with a Ruger Mark III 22/45. By time we were done both father and son were hooked.

From the range I took them to the local gun shop, and he bought his son an airsoft pistol. The next day he went out on his own and bought two pistols for himself. He shared with me what caused his transition, how he'd gone from a totally gun-free home to a man ready to buy two guns and sign up for a concealed carry class.

He told me that a few days prior, in his own neighborhood, there had been a home invasion. An elderly couple in their eighties had been shot to death. It was a low-crime, upscale community. His son heard about it and came to him and asked, "Dad, what happens if they break into our house?"

My friend didn't have an answer for his son. And that's when he called me. Damn it feels good to reel in a convert!

The anti-gunners are in a tizzy right now, because the NRA just got 250,000 new members on the heels of a school shooting; and because guns are flying off shelves; and because the ammo store cupboards are bare. They're scratching their heads saying, "What the hell just happened?"

Well, it's Barack Obama, stupid! Every time the man opens his mouth people buy more guns. And now that he's proposing gun bans and registration, the anti-gunners don't stand a prayer. The big question here is why? Why, on the heels of a terrible tragedy like the Sandy Hook elementary shooting where twenty little kids were murdered, are people running out and arming themselves with guns as fast as they can?

It's simple. Because most people care about their families. Obama's an anti-gunner, but his kids are protected by dozens of guns and guards. Even the liberals know the only way to stop a bad guy with a gun is with a good guy with a gun. So even while they rail against guns they make sure there are plenty around them and their families. It's common sense.

So let them keep proposing gun control all they want. They are unifying the 2A troops; our ranks are swelling; many who were on the fence are rapidly jumping over to our side.

You might ask me, "Skip, you seem optimistic in the midst of a full-on frontal assault on the Second Amendment. Is there any chance of us losing more of our freedom?" My answer: "Damn straight there is."

But quite frankly I prefer an open fight. Let's duke it out now rather than drag it on for generations to come. This is one old warrior who loves the smell of gun smoke whether it's literal or figurative.

Here's what I say: "Bring it on, Bammy! Molon Labe! Come and take them!" But whatever you do, don't stop shooting your mouth off, because the more you talk the more people see you for the fool you are and buy more guns.

But the most important thing is this: Now my friend has an answer for his 10-year-old son. And it goes something like this: "Don't worry, son. If someone tries to hurt you, I'll double-tap center of exposed mass until he stops."

And that makes sense whether you're a banker, a redneck or even the anti-gun President of the United States.

ABOUT THE AUTHOR

Skip Coryell lives with his wife and children in Michigan. Skip Coryell is the author of nine books including *Blood in the Streets: Concealed Carry and the OK Corral*, *RKBA: Defending the Right to Keep and Bear Arms*, *The God Virus*, and *We Hold These Truths*. He is the founder of The Second Amendment March, a Marine Corps veteran, and the President of White Feather Press. He is an avid hunter and sportsman, a Marine Corps veteran, and a graduate of Cornerstone University. For more details on Skip Coryell, or to contact him personally, go to his website at skipcoryell.com

To get a copy of Skip's latest novel *The Shadow Militia*, go to store.whitefeatherpress.com or amazon. com.

Disarming the citizens is ALWAYS done piecemeal. It's how Creeping T (creeping tyranny) occurs. Law by law. Precept by precept. Fiat by fiat. Decree by decree. Until we begin to reflect the very captivity our forefathers died to prevent.

THE FEEL GOOD +
THE STEAL GOOD = CAPTIVITY

Written By Audrey Russo

18 January 2013

> *"They that can give up essential liberty to obtain a little temporary safety deserve neither liberty nor safety."*
>
> *– Benjamin Franklin, Historical Review of Pennsylvania, 1759*

In the wake of the Newtown, CT shooting, leaders across the nation (specifically Democrat) have focused on the Constitution. Not to uphold it, but rather to find a way to violate it without the knowledge of the electorate (present company excepted).

Now, allow me to preface my opinion with this: All crime that destroys innocent life is wrong. I'm using comparisons to make a point. And, due to the axiomatic lingo, I'm forced to refer to people here as black or white. That said…

Chicago, IL, Obama's adopted hometown, had the highest murder rate in the nation last year. The 2012 number was 513. Higher than any other State in the Union. The majority of those murders were black-on-black. Black thugs, with illegal guns, killing unarmed, law-abiding black citizens.

So, here's a question: Why the hue and cry for whites murdering white people, but not a mention of black-on-black crime?

It seems that mass murderers are always white. But, if someone of African descent committed the crime in Newtown, would we even be talking about this right now? The answer is unequivocally NO.

Why? Because the Liberal media is permanently plagued with a fatal case of White Guilt, which never has an equitable result. Anything done out of guilt never has a profitable outcome, but rather ends up exacerbating the problem.

The MSM won't mention black-on-black crime out of fear of being labeled racist (something they often employ on their opposition). Yet, thousands of innocent Americans of darker skin hue who … thanks to a combination of those with a penchant for the Ruling Class (Marxists) and those who live by emotion (Liberals) … are prevented from protecting themselves from these miscreants. And this, as in all things liberal, emboldens the criminals.

With no fingerprints, they are able to keep blacks killing blacks at an alarming rate … and assure thugs that they can rape, pillage and kill because the law-abiding are defenseless. Then whip the masses into a cry for even more restrictions on their rights. And…

We have a winner!!. The joining of these two forces: Liberals (the "Feel Good" crowd) and Marxists (the "Steal Good'" crowd), are both targeting the Second Amendment. And putting all other rights aside: Without the right of self-defense, all other rights are moot!

The empirical evidence, when factored into the discourse, always bolsters the right of the citizen to bear arms. Not for hunting … as Libs love to parrot … but rather for self-defense, as the Framers intended.

The rush to legislation (or Executive Orders) that is now taking place, will further UNDERMINE liberty and embolden the nefarious, now strutting like peacocks. The Feel Good crowd has succeeded in making citizens feel bad about the only thing that stands between them and tyrants/criminals: Guns.

Noah Webster once said, in An Examination of the Leading Principles of the Federal Constitution (Philadelphia 1787):

Before a standing army can rule, the people must be disarmed; as they are in almost every kingdom in Europe. The supreme power in America cannot enforce unjust laws by the sword; because the whole body of the people are armed, and constitute a force superior to any band of regular troops that can be, on any pretence, raised in the United States. A military force, at the command of Congress, can execute no laws, but such as the people perceive to be just and constitutional; for they will possess the power, and jealousy will instantly inspire the inclination, to resist the execution of a law which appears to them unjust and oppressive.

Disarming the citizens is ALWAYS done piecemeal. It's how Creeping T (creeping tyranny) occurs. Law by law. Precept by precept. Fiat by fiat. Decree by decree. Until we begin to reflect the very captivity our forefathers died to prevent.

Protecting the Second Amendment, protects your freedom. Praise the Lord and pass the ammunition!

ABOUT THE AUTHOR

Audrey Russo is the Host of the weekly REELTalk Radio Show and the co-host of WOMANTalk Radio Show. She handles Middle East Issues/National Security/Terrorism for their eZine and writes on foreign affairs for The Examiner.com. She guests on several radio shows including The Rick Amato Show, The Simon Conway Show, The Pat Campbell Show and The Mike Wiley Show. Audrey is the Managing Editor for the online opinion journal Ediblog. com. Her articles can also be read at The Center for Changing Worldviews and the Gold Coast Chronicle as well as other online journals. She is also an active member of the NYC performing arts community as a singer and actor.

Individuals that are fundamentally opposed to owning a fire-arm shall be taxed and each year shall register with the government as firearms objectors until age 62 or until proven by a medical doctor to be unable to operate a firearm.

PROJECT AMENDMENT 28 – AMEND THE CONSTITUTION FOR COMMON SENSE GUN OWNERSHIP

Written By Mike Piccione

18 January 2013

Let me be the first to suggest a common sense gun regulation that will include and accommodate all Americans. Every able bodied individual in America should be required to own a gun.

In the recent American political tradition of justifying something because that is how a European country does it, I suggest we follow the Swiss. Not only do they love their watches and chocolate, they also love their guns. They love guns so much their government picks up the tab to ensure that people own them and form militias. That's right, government funded civilian militias are the foundation of the most peaceful of European countries.

Swiss people are given Sig's, mostly Sig SG 550's. Now that is an assault rifle. A real assault rifle – the fully automatic kind – not the one-shot-per-pull of the trigger semi-automatic rifles Americans own.

Officers have the Sig Sauer P-220 in .45 ACP in their homes. That ACP stands for Automatic Colt Pistol. Our American military is reduced to having the 9mm Parabellum. In an ironic twist of fate the non-warring Swiss opted for a powerful American handgun cartridge for their government sponsored civilian militia and we war loving Americans opted for a much weaker European handgun cartridge for our government sponsored military. Swiss civilians are issued stronger handguns than the American military. Mull that over for a while.

The Swiss Embrace Their Civilian Militia

The Federal Constitution of the Swiss Confederation article 58 states: Switzerland shall have armed forces. In principle, the armed forces shall be organized as a militia.

All Swiss men get military training except for those who have opted for an alternative civilian service. If you do neither military nor civilian service you get taxed. After getting your Swiss Army training you go home and become part of the militia for the next 10 years or so, and your gun goes with you.

Guns and Crime

I think we all know by now that crime in the United States and gun control laws have a direct correlation. Chicago, Detroit and Washington, D.C. are all gun control cities where you are more likely to get killed than in either of our theaters of war.

Kennesaw, Georgia requires gun ownership. In 2007, the city was selected by *Family Circle* magazine as one of the nation's "10 best towns for families."

In 1982 the Municipal Code of Kennesaw, Georgia was changed to state:

(a) In order to provide for the emergency management of the city, and further in order to provide for and protect the safety, security and general welfare of the city and its inhabitants, every head of household residing in the city limits is required to maintain a firearm, together with ammunition therefore.

(b) Exempt from the effect of this section are those heads of households who suffer a physical or mental disability which would prohibit them from using such a firearm. Further exempt from the effect of this section are those heads of households who are paupers or who conscientiously oppose maintaining firearms as a result of beliefs or religious doctrine, or persons convicted of a felony.

Guess what happened after the ordinance was passed. Crime dropped. Much to the displeasure of anti-gun groups that promised the people would suddenly become drunk with blood lust and shoot each other. It never happened. Peace broke out and civility was waged among the people.

The Common Sense Solution – Amend the Constitution

The last time America amended the Constitution was in 1992. Who knew eh? Here is the gutsy and bold addition to our most precious of founding documents:

> *No law, varying the compensation for the services of the Senators and Representatives, shall take effect, until an election of Representatives shall have intervened.*

I think it has something to do with Congress giving Congress a raise. It took 202 years to get it passed. Amazing.

Our 28th Amendment shall be:

> *In order to provide for the security of the individual, state and general wellbeing of the country, all able bodied individuals shall be required to own one modern firearm and a minimum of ten rounds of associated ammunition.*

> *Individuals are required to receive training in marksmanship and operation of firearms. Military and law enforcement personnel shall be exempt from training if they have satisfactorily completed firearms training while in the course of their service.*

> *Exceptions shall be made for those adjudicated mentally ill, convicted of a crime of domestic violence, a felony, or have been separated from the military with a Dishonorable Discharge.*

> *Individuals that are fundamentally opposed to owning a firearm shall be taxed and each year shall register with the government as firearms objectors until age 62 or until proven by a medical doctor to be unable to operate a firearm.*

> *If an individual is unable to purchase a firearm one shall be provided by the Federal Government.*

Next Steps

We need to get this up as a petition to the White House. Then we will need 100,000 signatures. From there we enthusiastically encourage our Congresspersons, Senators and Governors to move this legislation forward.

I'd be honored to have it referred to as the *Piccione Gun Safety Amendment* but my name is hard to pronounce.

Let's just call it *Project Amendment 28* and make this the 28th Amendment to the Constitution of the United States.

It makes common sense to adopt this reasonable approach to securing our country and accommodate those that choose not to do their fair share. Common sense and fair share – principles we can all embrace.

ABOUT THE AUTHOR

Mike Piccione is the Guns & Gear editor for the Daily Caller.

Men should be carrying the weight of the church on their strong backs and leading in gentleness and humility. Serving the women and children not abusing them. The answer is for the Fathers to turn their hearts back to their children.

AMERICA'S ROOT PROBLEM: A CULTURE OF FATHERLESSNESS

Written By John Renken

18 January 2013

> *Malachi 4:6 And he will turn the hearts of fathers to their children and the hearts of children to their fathers, lest I come and strike the land with a decree of utter destruction.*

In case you haven't noticed there is an epidemic in our churches and in our nation. I mean this both literally and figuratively. I don't think for a second that it is an exaggeration to point to the single most important reason we are losing ground. The reason we are losing ground is because we have lost the men!

In his excellent book *Why Men Hate Going to Church*, David Murrow's research finds that 60% of church attendance across denominational lines is women. Look at your own church. Who are the majority of attenders? Take it a step further, who are the majority of volunteer leadership? Who teaches the majority of your Sunday school classes? It is women unless your church is the exception to the rule.

This particular epidemic isn't just a church problem but, as I alluded to earlier, this is a problem in our nation. When we look at our educational system we must admit that the vast majority of teachers are females. Peg Tyre in her article *"The Trouble with Boys"* shows us that boys are having more difficulties in school as the teaching methodologies utilized primarily suit girls. She concludes that:

> *One of the most reliable predictors of whether a boy will succeed or fail in high school rests on a single question: does he have a man in his life to look up to? Too often, the answer is no. High rates of divorce and single*

motherhood have created a generation of fatherless boys. In every kind of neighborhood, rich or poor, an increasing number of boys – now a startling 40 percent – are being raised without their biological dads.

There are tons of signs of the trouble we are facing as a nation and in our churches. Some of those signs are very startling statistics.

- 63% of youth suicides are from fatherless homes (US Dept. Of Health/Census) – 5 times the average.

- 90% of all homeless and runaway children are from fatherless homes – 32 times the average.

- 85% of all children who show behavior disorders come from fatherless homes – 20 times the average. (Center for Disease Control)

- 80% of rapists with anger problems come from fatherless homes –14 times the average. (Justice & Behavior, Vol 14, p. 403-26)

- 71% of all high school dropouts come from fatherless homes – 9 times the average. (National Principals Association Report)

- 70% of youths in state-operated institutions come from fatherless homes – 9 times the average. (U.S. Dept. of Justice, Sept. 1988)

- 85% of all youths in prison come from fatherless homes – 20 times the average. (Fulton Co. Georgia, Texas Dept. of Correction)

- 71% of pregnant teenagers lack a father. [U.S. Department of Health and Human Services press release, Friday, March 26, 1999]

- 75% of adolescent patients in chemical abuse centers come from fatherless homes. [Rainbows f for all God's Children]

- 70% of juveniles in state operated institutions have no father. [US Department of Justice, Special Report, Sept. 1988]

- 85% of youths in prisons grew up in a fatherless home. [Fulton County Georgia jail populations, Texas Department of Corrections, 1992]

After reading those horrifying statistics you should be awake by now and asking what is the answer? The answer is for churches to begin to target men like Jesus did. Then those churches should begin discipling those men and then put those men in leadership!

Men should be carrying the weight of the church on their strong backs and leading in gentleness and humility. Serving the women and children not abusing them. The answer is for the Fathers to turn their hearts back to their children.

Mark Driscoll, one of the most influential men in America, discusses the issue of going after men in this video clip.

About the Author

A self proclaimed "scrapper" since childhood, John Renken grew up with a burning interest in physical challenges and a strong competitive spirit which has led him to develop quite an impressive reputation in the professional fighting community. Reaching the pinnacle of his career, Renken now has over 68 professional mixed martial arts and boxing matches under his belt and many first place titles spanning three different continents. A former Satanist, Renken's life has taken many interesting twists and turns along the way to redemption. He now pastors a church called Freedom Church and writes about topics of interest in our country.

First off, dipsticks, the Second Amendment has nada to do with hunting. The Founding Fathers weren't worried about their right to put the bam to Bambi (although we should be because progressives hate hunting and would love nothing more than to bring that activity to a grinding halt).

When I Want a Progressive's Opinion on What Guns I Should Have/Hunt with, I'll Give it to Them

Written By Doug Giles

20 January 2013

My buddy, Green Beret badass Bryan Sikes, shot a massive whitetail buck last week during our South Texas Purple Heart Adventure. He whacked said muy grande with a LaRue Tactical OBR chambered for the glorious .308 Win. round. Oh and BTW, Sikes used a high capacity magazine during this hunt.

For those of you who aren't hip to the LaRue, it is a weapon that progressive darlings say we should not have because we don't "need" such a weapon for hunting.

Hunting, according to these wizards of odd, is what they think our Founding Fathers had in mind when they penned that pesky Second Amendment, and according to these control freaks we don't need a tactical weapon with a high capacity magazine to hunt with.

First off, dipsticks, the Second Amendment has nada to do with hunting. The Founding Fathers weren't worried about their right to put the bam to Bambi (although we should be because progressives hate hunting and would love nothing more than to bring that activity to a grinding halt). If you don't believe me, just corner one of these little darlings and ask them what they think about hunting.

Secondly, who are they to tell us what we "need" or don't need when it comes to anything? Typical of the Left, they think they know what's best for we the people. If you want to talk about "needs," Ms. Leftist, we don't need iPhones, Porsches, crazy straws, American Idol, beer, leaf blowers, and I don't need a gorgeous Italian wife. But that's America, folks. Stay out of our business.

Regarding the need for high capacity magazines for hunting, please tell the ranchers in the west when they're doing depredation work on predators and nuisance animals that they don't need such weapons. You might be surprised.

Now, for the record, I do not have a black weapon. I'm a bolt action, lever action, double rifle, and traditional side-by-side shotgun freak. I like the classic lines of beautiful sporting guns.

However, the more I contemplate our current milieu I'm beginning to think that a semi-auto, like the LaRue Tactical chambered for the .308, has got to be the ultimate gun. Why? Well, it's quite effective on game up to moose, and it has been proven in battle against tyrants—which is exactly what the Second Amendment is all about, namely, whacking overreaching, freedom-strangling little King George wannabes should they oppress.

About Doug Giles

Doug Giles is the man behind ClashDaily.com. In addition to driving ClashDaily.com, Giles is a popular columnist on Townhall.com and the author of the book Raising Righteous & Rowdy Girls.

Doug's articles have also appeared on several other print and online news sources, including The Washington Times, The Daily Caller, Fox Nation, USA Today, The Wall Street Journal, The Washington Examiner, The Blaze, American Hunter Magazine and ABC News.

He's been a frequent guest on the Fox News Channel and Fox Business Channel as well as many nationally syndicated radio shows across the nation — which, he believes, officially makes him a super hero.

In addition, Doug is an occasional guest host on New York City's WABC (The Jason Mattera Show) and he is a weekly guest, every Friday at 7:45am[et], on America's Morning News (155 markets).

Giles and his wife Margaret have two daughters: Hannah, who devastated ACORN with her 2009 nation shaking undercover videos, and Regis who is an NRA columnist, huntress and Second Amendment activist.

DG's interests include guns, big game hunting, big game fishing, fine art, cigars, helping wounded warriors, and being a big pain in the butt to people who dislike God and the USA.

Read more Doug Giles at www.clashdaily.com.

It is only through anonymity and symbolism that this foe can be engaged effectively. If the drug lords do not know who their enemy is, they cannot defend against him.

Mexican Heroes: A Glimmer of Hope in the Fight Against the Cartels

Written By Luke Hamilton

24 January 2013

If you kick a man enough times, sometimes you draw back a stump. And the Mexican drug cartels have been doing a lot of kicking. In rural areas of Mexico, far away from the spotlight of international media and high-profile arrests, the problem of violent drug thugs is being dealt with in an unconventional manner. In the southwestern state of Guererro, citizens are taking to the streets, masked and armed. They are determined to do what the local and national governments have been unable to do: protect innocent civilians.

Since 2006, there have been nearly 70,000 people killed nationwide and residents in the municipalities of Ayutia de los Libres and Teconoapa have had enough. For the past couple of weeks, 800 locals have volunteered to serve as a makeshift militia, setting up checkpoints, enforcing curfews, and arresting alleged criminals. They are not trained or well-armed, but they are determined to correct what their corrupt government has failed to do.

They have announced that they've arrested 44 criminals thus far and insist that they will handle justice internally, judging the cases of these criminals with a committee formed from the municipalities involved. Are there potential civil rights violations possible in a situation like this? Of course, but this is not the relevant question. Are there already civil rights violations happening on a daily (if not hourly) basis in Mexico? The answer is a resounding yes. If a community in danger exercises its right to defend itself, I say "¡Bueno!"

In today's progressive world, the ability of everyday citizens to do nearly anything with any competence is viewed with skepticism and scorn. "That should be left to the experts.." is heard time and again, while we are left with an emasculated population, growing increasingly distrustful of its own ability to do anything! This liberal hyperventilation is clearly seen in our national firearm dialogue. Progressives are aghast at the thought that average, everyday Americans could be trusted to handle weapons which are used by our military. The thought that dirt-poor, frustrated Mexican farmers would be competent enough to handle law enforcement and a penal code likely has scores of defense attorneys frantically shifting their vacation plans to the Caribbean, where the population is more complacent about federal fecklessness.

I always say, if Macbeth and Scarface have taught us anything it is that powerful men have powerful fears (which are usually amplified by the use of drugs and/or witchcraft). Will the counter-offensive launched by poor Mexican farmers be successful? Only time will tell. Traditional tactical thinking would always discourage engaging with an enemy which possesses such a vast superiority in firepower, however this situation is anything but traditional. The advantage of superior firepower disappears when you have no target at which to aim.

In a strange way, the Mexican vigilantes are taking a page from the Dark Knight's playbook. The police cannot fight this foe effectively. They can be targeted and eliminated too easily, through murder or bribery. It is only through anonymity and symbolism that this foe can be engaged effectively. If the drug lords do not know who their enemy is, they cannot defend against him.

They might send their product along a new route, to avoid a potential ambush along the way, but there is no way to guarantee that the man they hired to drive the truck hasn't been affected by the murderous marauding of his employers, to the point that he becomes a sympathizer. Yes, the Cocainistas can keep their inner circle tight, but living the life of a most-wanted drug lord requires a lot of little people to turn the gears, and these animals have made a sport of terrorizing the little people. With any luck, there is a Jael or two amongst the staff of these mansions, biding her time.

As R'as al Ghul teaches Bruce Wayne, symbolism can be more effective than reality. The symbol of the masked farmer is more powerful than the masked farmer himself. A man can be defeated but a symbol cannot. While these 800 men might wither under the fire of a truck-mounted 50-cal, the message they are sending is their most powerful weapon. If this homespun militia takes root in Mexico, it will be because these men picked up rusty shotguns in trembling hands and took a stand. "In less than a month, they have done something that the army and state and federal police haven't been able to do in years," said local resident Lorena Morales Castro, "They are our anonymous heroes."

About the Author

Luke Hamilton is a part-time columnist, part-time actor, full-time patriot. In addition to ClashDaily, he currently writes for uncommonshow.com and has performed on stage in Chicago and his native stomping ground of Eugene, Oregon.

I am now 'Hamid al-Pierre,' not 'Wayne LaPierre.' And yes, if Obama wants to go after four and a half million gun owners, all of whom are now becoming devout Muslims, then the government can expect the biggest discrimination lawsuit ever.

La Pierre's Bold Move: NRISLAM

Written By Nick Taxia

29 January 2013

Publisher's Note: The following piece is satire. I repeat - the following piece is satirical in nature. (That means it's not really true and the author just wrote it for fun.) Reach up and flick the switch on your head labeled "HUMOR". You won't regret it.

by D'Leereeus Johnson, DP staff

Tuesday, January 29th, 2013

(FAIRFAX, VA) — "How do ya' like me now?!" the National Rifle Association effectively said.

Last Wednesday. Reacting to the Obama administration's executive orders to curb gun violence and "suggestions" on how to prevent further incidents like the Newtown massacre, NRA CEO and Executive Vice President, Wayne LaPierre announced yesterday that he and the entire membership of the National Rifle Association were converting to Islam.

The stunning declaration is being condemned as "cowardly" by some gun rights supporters and "brilliantly strategic and practical" by others, as the nation's biggest pro-gun organization now all being Muslims will no doubt stave off the administration's attempts to tighten controls on gun owners (the rationale being that via the NRA's being Muslim, hence a notoriously downtrodden minority, the White House and allies in Congress would not dare move to take away their rights to own firearms of whatever magnitude; such moves would be discriminatory if not out-right racist, claims the NRA).

"This administration loves providing guns — big guns, and thousands of them — to Muslim fighters in Libya, Egypt, now Syria," said LaPierre, bedecked in Wahhabi-style Muslim garb, at a press conference last Wednesday. "Many of these rebel groups consist of radical jihadists who hate America just as much as the governments we're helping them topple. If Obama is so pro-gun when it comes to radical Muslims, then damn it, we at the NRA are now radical Muslims, too!"

When asked by reporters if he and the rest of the NRA's 4.5 million members actually expected to be taken seriously, believing the administration would find their change of faith too intimidating to continue curtailing legal gun ownership, LaPierre snapped, "First, I am now 'Hamid al-Pierre,' not 'Wayne LaPierre.' And yes, if Obama wants to go after four and a half million gun owners, all of whom are now becoming devout Muslims, then the government can expect the biggest discrimination lawsuit ever. ... And also we urge all non-NRA gun owners in America to convert to Islam, or declare themselves gay, or make whatever changes it takes to place them in a more 'politically correct group.' Thereby a more 'protected' group."

According to 2010 census statistics, the average NRA member is Caucasian, male, age 35 to 65, of working class, Protestant, and suburban and rural dwelling.

Furthermore, all registered gun owners, NRA members or not, make up a wider range of demographics, however they still generally reflect those of the NRA, a fact the now "Hamid al-Pierre" was not shy in discussing.

"It is unmistakable," continued al-Pierre through a scraggly, grayish-black beard and noticeably darker skin, "most of us legal gun owners in America belong to its least 'politically correct' group. So if we just change as many aspects of ourselves, we should stop the administration's efforts to thwart our Second Amendment rights dead in their tracks."

Although an astute AP reporter was quick to point out that al-Pierre was of French and English decent, al-Pierre retorted, "There's gotta be some Middle-Eastern or African ancestry in my family somewhere ...I'm looking into it. In any case, I've been hitting the tanning bed pretty hard. And I urge all our members out there to start doing the same! Allahu Akbar!"

<u>Obama Administration Reacts to "Cowardly" NRA Conversion Tactic</u>

With the nation's attention focused last Wednesday on Secretary of State Hillary Clinton's long awaited testimony on the September 11th terror attacks in Benghazi (also by radical Muslims), little was paid to White House Press Secretary James Carney's response to the NRA's announcement/conversion at his daily briefing.

"Admittedly, we're perplexed at the (NRA's) announcement of its conversion to Islam," said a stunned-looking Carney. "And if more legal gun owners follow the NRA's lead and convert to Islam, it will make it even harder for the administration to push for tighter gun laws, since we all know it's middle-aged, rural, Christian white men with families who legally own guns who are the greatest threat in America today. Now we've lost much of that dangerous demographic.

It's a strategically cowardly move."

Said Larry Pratt, Director of Gun Owners of America, NRA's top rival group, "This is the sleaziest, cheapest maneuver to avoid confronting the gun-grabbers in America and the White House," said Pratt following the al-Pierre's announcement Wednesday morning. "We should be challenging these anti-Second Amendment folks head-on, not changing our religions to make ourselves into 'minorities' and more 'PC-appealing'!"

But NRA members are following Hamid al-Pierre's example, researching compatible Islamic names, area mosques and customs. Knoxville, Tennessee resident and father of four, Albert Sherman, said he will be formally changing his name to Muhammad Ali Shermad-Shabbaz. "My wife and I own several guns, including an AR-15, and we'll all be converting to Islam within a week and visiting our local mosque ... if there is one in Tennessee."

"After all," added the 54-year-old commercial property renovator, "there was no 'national debate' about guns when a crazed Muslim kid shot and killed five at the Trolley Square mall in 2007 while screaming 'Allahu Akbar,' just like there was no national debate when Nidal Hassan murdered 13 fellow soldiers at Fort Hood while screaming 'God Is Great' either."

"I just don't know how I'll ever give up bacon," said a somber Mrs. soon-to-be Shermad-Shabbaz, thinking of her future as a Muslim wife. "We eat bacon every day. We even have bacon ice cream!"

However, if giving up bacon is the worst she must endure to secure her family's right to bear arms, Mrs. Sherman, 55, said it is something she can live with. "We'll deal with no bacon, but that also means no sharia law in our house, either! Albert wouldn't impose 'sharia' on me or our (two) daughters. And he couldn't even if he tried."

When asked why her husband couldn't impose strict Islamic codes in their house, Sherman replied, "Simple: I'll blow his weiner off.

ABOUT THE AUTHOR

Nick Taxia is a former campaign manager and consultant in Washington, D.C. He is the primary writer and producer of the conservative-leaning satirical web site, DuhProgressive.com, as well as a rising radio personality, commentator, and comedian.

I'm not beyond sticking a pair of scissors into a murderer's skull if that's my only recourse, but I still think a gun would be a better weapon —just like our president once said while campaigning: "Never bring a knife to a gun fight." If the DHS wants to play "Glock, paper, scissors" with my life, I'm going for Glock every time.

Armed Guard Saves School Last Week (Gun Control Freaks Wrong Again)

Written By Doug Giles

3 February 2013

Vice President Biden unfurled his genius during a Google+ "fireside" hangout last month stating that having "armed guards in schools would be a terrible mistake."

Really, José? Why don't you rock up to Price Middle School in Atlanta on Monday morning and bray that insanity to the teachers and students who were spared an early grave because an armed guard took out the murderous wannabe before he could waylay his peers?

Oh, I'm sorry. Y'all haven't heard about the armed guard taking down a shooter who passed his gun through the metal detectors at an Atlanta middle school? My bad. I forgot that the Lamestream Media doesn't report on commonsense solutions to potential mass murders. It doesn't fit the fables they're trying to foist upon us, ergo they give it dog meat during the evening "news." God … I'm so stupid to assume that you had heard about it. I'll never learn. Click the link in the second paragraph if you want the lowdown on this situation, which totally validates the no-duh fact that a gun in the hands of a good dude stops bad guys before things get ugly. Durrrrrrrr.

Anyway, back to Biden and his ilk's brilliance on combating mass murderers. Biden said that not only do we not need armed guards in schools and that such a thing would be a mistake, but he also chimed in that what schools really need is a more robust staff of shrinks to dissuade Scooter, Jr. from strafing his mates.

Not wanting to be out-Bidened, this week the DHS rolled out an instructional video that counseled those in a mass-shooting scenario to …

Number one: Call 911. Okay, this is generally a good idea. However, bear in mind that the average number of people killed by a mass murderer by the time the law has finally arrived is about fourteen. The average number of people killed when an armed civilian is there is 2.5. Thanks, DHS, for looking out for us. Remember, folks: When seconds count, the police are minutes away. Yep, the average response time for the police to get to such a situation is around five minutes … and the average response time of my .357 magnum shooting Hornady's 125gr. FXT Critical Defense rounds out of my S&W Airlite is 1,200 feet per second.

Number two: Hide under the desk. Correct me if I'm wrong, but I believe that the Virginia Tech tool who killed many co-eds shot them while they cowered under their desks. Cowering under a desk, playing opossum, is not the way this cowboy wants to be remembered. I think this is what is called the "Pussification" of the American male.

Number three: Use scissors. Another thing that floored me in the video was the DHS advising those who are forced to field such a crappy conundrum to pick up some scissors and confront the culprit. Scissors? Really? What kind of scissors, Janet? Pinking shears or Floyd the barber's clippers? Look, I'm not beyond sticking a pair of scissors into a murderer's skull if that's my only recourse, but I still think a gun would be a better weapon —just like our president once said while campaigning: "Never bring a knife to a gun fight." If the DHS wants to play "Glock, paper, scissors" with my life, I'm going for Glock every time.

You know the Left yarbles on and on about how precious our children are and how they want to protect the kids, but they think armed guards on our campuses is oh, so cave-mannish. Meanwhile, they protect the president, congressmen, governors, and celebrities; they protect sporting events, jewelry stores, gold caches, banks, office buildings, factories and courts with guns, yet they defend our kids with "Gun Free Zone" signs and recommend teachers use scissors. Pardon my French, parents, but you're bat crap crazy and these mass shootings will go on and on if you keep listening to the asininities of the lunatic Left.

About Doug Giles

Doug Giles is the man behind ClashDaily.com. In addition to driving ClashDaily.com, Giles is a popular columnist on Townhall.com and the author of the book Raising Righteous & Rowdy Girls.

Doug's articles have also appeared on several other print and online news sources, including The Washington Times, The Daily Caller, Fox Nation, USA Today, The Wall Street Journal, The Washington Examiner, The Blaze, American Hunter Magazine and ABC News.

He's been a frequent guest on the Fox News Channel and Fox Business Channel as well as many nationally syndicated radio shows across the nation — which, he believes, officially makes him a super hero.

In addition, Doug is an occasional guest host on New York City's WABC (The Jason Mattera Show) and he is a weekly guest, every Friday at 7:45am[et], on America's Morning News (155 markets).

Giles and his wife Margaret have two daughters: Hannah, who devastated ACORN with her 2009 nation shaking undercover videos, and Regis who is an NRA columnist, huntress and Second Amendment activist.

DG's interests include guns, big game hunting, big game fishing, fine art, cigars, helping wounded warriors, and being a big pain in the butt to people who dislike God and the USA.

Read more Doug Giles at www.clashdaily.com.

EPILOGUE

* On January 31st 2012 The Newtown Board of Education asked the town to make room for more armed police officers in its budget. They requested one additional armed officer at each of the town's four elementary schools. The request was approved. The officers will be Newtown police officers. "Our parents are demanding of us that things are made safe and secure and certain measures are put in place," said Chairwoman Debbie Leidlein. "So we're being very thoughtful."

- source: http://www.nbcconnecticut.com/news/local/Newtown-Votes-for-Armed-School-Officers-189320221.html?dr

White
Feather
Press

Other hard-hitting books in defense of the Second Amendment by White Feather Press

Raising Righteous and Rowdy Girls (Doug Giles)
RKBA: Defending the Right to Keep and Bear Arms (Skip Coryell)
Lessons from Armed America (Kathy Jackson & Mark Walters)
Raising Boys Feminists Will Hate (Doug Giles)
Stalking Natalie (Skip Coryell)
By Force of Patriots (Cameron Reddy)
The Cornered Cat: A Woman's Guide to Concealed Carry (Kathy Jackson)
Blood in the Streets: Concealed Carry and the OK Corral (Skip Coryell)
My Parents Open Carry (Brian Jeffs & Nathan Nephew)
In Due Time (JK Jones)
America's History is His Story (RG Yoho)